Praise for ...

"Skilled communication in business is key to success. Orlaith shares a wealth of insight, based on deep experience, so helpful for anyone starting out or progressing further in their career."
– Liam Casey, CEO, PCH International

"As the future of work evolves, and hybrid working becomes more embedded, personal communication skills are more important than ever. This book will help you develop those skills."
– Anne O'Leary, VP EMEA, Meta

"A great book for new business entrants, you only get one chance to make a first impression, so with Orlaith's help you are on the right track"
– Larry Bass, Television Producer, CEO at ShinAwiL, Dublin

"Orlaith is exactly the type of communicator I most admire, strong and influential, but also authentic and empathetic. Everyone can learn from this book."
– Tammy Darcy Founder and CEO, The Shona Project

"Learning to communicate well is a key requirement for success in business. Orlaith's book will help anyone looking to improve their communication skills."
– Barry O'Sullivan, Senior Advisor at Permira, Palo Alto, California

Other books by the author:

Without You - Living With Loss
Perform As A Leader

SPEAK NOW

Communicate Well in the Workplace

ORLAITH CARMODY

First published in 2015 by Ballpoint Press as
Perform As A Leader
www.ballpointpress.ie

2nd revised edition published in 2022 by Tara Press as:
Speak Now – Communicate Well in the Workplace
www.TaraPress.net

ISBN 978-1-9999262-4-3

Author portrait: Barry McCall
Book design by: Cyberscribe.eu
Printed and bound by Sprintprint, Dublin

DEDICATION

For Blathnaid

Contents

Introduction

When I brought out the first edition of this book, *Perform As A Leader*, there was a conversation underway in business and public circles about the impending leadership shortage the world over. The chatter was all about the leadership gap, and how it would be filled, with baby-boomers retiring in their thousands, taking away with them heads stuffed full of knowledge and experience.

Would those on the way up the ladder see a big opportunity to grasp the nettle, acquire the skills and step up to the plate? Or would the very different styles of working evidently preferred by younger generations prevail, to the point where leadership roles were not the goal they used to be?

If there is one thing clear about the significant changes in working patterns we have seen in recent years it is that people expect - and indeed deserve - a different kind of working life, a lot less about long hours and rote contribution, and a lot more about purpose, personal development and fulfilment.

The Covid-19 pandemic flung it all into high relief. Work life balance landed into our worlds, with remote or hybrid working firstly a necessity, and then quickly becoming the optimum for many people.

The way we work today has undergone more change in a few short years than in many of the previous decades all rolled together. Companies or concerns that don't offer flexibility will struggle to recruit, and indeed to promote in cases where a step-up results in benefits lost, or where the new role demands a presenteeism that might be considered unacceptable.

Communicating successfully in the workplace is more important than ever, and while I believed much of the content of the original to be evergreen, the book needed a complete overhaul, with lots to be taken out, but lots of exciting new material to be added in.

None of us is ever fully cooked, and I am no exception. Despite what I thought I knew before, I have learned loads more in the last few years which I have tried to capture here, and hope you find it helpful as you plot your career trajectory.

So the focus of this version of the book is less on leadership, which you may or may not aspire to, and more on the practical communication skills that every workplace requires, and which can be applied from wherever you happen to be working – in person, at home, or in the boat or holiday home if you are very lucky!

The core content is the same as the previous version, I like to think it is dateless. But I have added lots about online and remote working, to make sure that you connect with your audience to the best of your ability from whatever platform you choose.

I see it as a huge positive that we have had to learn to navigate poor wi-fi signals and interruptions from dogs barking and kids looking for biscuits. It brings out the very best in a presenter or meeting contributor when you have to stay cool regardless of what is going on around you. Although at this stage of the game, I advocate for planning well to ensure those interruptions are kept to a minimum. Our patience with them waned somewhat as time went on!

But if we want hybrid and remote working to stay - and most of us do it would seem - we each have to do our bit to be as professional as possible, as often as possible. Without ever losing that lovely warmth and connection we discovered, often by accident, when learning how to teach, or present, or conduct a webinar, or participate in a meeting online.

The world of work is rapidly evolving, and we all have to keep up to speed. Improving your ability to present and speak in public, pitch your business, do a good interview, run a good meeting, conduct a strong negotiation or coach a team can do wonders for your career trajectory.

I hope you enjoy this slimmed down, souped up version of my original book, designed to bring lots of tried and tested techniques to a whole new audience. Thank you for choosing it, and I sincerely hope you achieve all the success you deserve.

Orlaith Carmody
December 2022

Chapter One

Connecting Onscreen

Reaching an audience and getting a message
across onscreen is about personality, connection,
and minimising distractions.

News anchor Bryan Dobson could be described as the Walter Cronkite of Irish broadcasting, so trusted his voice, so steady his presence across the years. I have been known to use his name when training.

"You know when Bryan is reading the news", I say to those wanting to improve their presentation skills, "the screen could go blank, the set behind could fall down, the studio could go on fire, and you just know that Bryan would say, don't worry folks, it is all under control."

And they all nod in complete agreement.

Because everyone knows that nothing, but nothing, could cause Bryan to lose a beat or miss a step. His calm confidence gives us, the viewers, comfort and reassurance, no matter how difficult the news might be that particular day.

It takes a huge talent, to display that level of screen presence, but there are things we can all learn from it, and techniques we can practice to make sure that we too connect as well as possible when speaking to remote individuals or groups from a laptop or other device. Before we explore the techniques involved in developing a presence onscreen that will allow you connect with an online audience confidently, let's take a look at why you need to consider this.

The rush to get online following the Covid-19 pandemic caught many sectors by surprise. For example a survey across higher education in Ireland in 2019, about the digital experience of teaching and learning, found that 70% of staff who teach in higher education had never done so in an online environment at that point.

70%! That's a huge portion of third level faculty members who, for one reason or another, were not really engaging with the potential of teaching online.

Galway academic Sharon Flynn of the Irish Universities Association was leading a digital transformation project in the seven universities the IUA covers, and says there had been plenty of investment in the technology. The facilities for recording lectures and for live sessions were in place, and training had been done.

But take-up had been low, with most teaching staff only dipping a toe in the water, by using the resources to provide back-up notes and additional material, rather than exploring the possibilities of using it as a primary or live teaching tool.

And then Covid struck, and within weeks, every single lecture offered by the seven universities had to be online. She describes what sounds like a kind of controlled pandemonium, where teams and resources were stretched to the absolute utmost to turn massive institutions around in days to ensure continuity of teaching.

And you know what? They succeeded, because they had no choice. They had to deliver, and get through from the first lockdown in mid-March 2020 to the end of term, pausing during the summer recess to re-group and then hit the ground running the following September.

In homes all over the world, at the same time, workers were frantically clearing space in spare bedrooms and on kitchen tables, as the lights went out in glass buildings, and city streets went silent. We were deeply shocked at first, and may have felt very strange talking to colleagues and trying to conduct our business or take our classes online, but we got used to it, and even more importantly, we got quite good at it. Practice does indeed make perfect.

I have spoken to thousands of people online in the last couple of years, ranging through online conventions with hundreds of people on board, mid-size groups on a webinar, small training or development groups, all the way to one on one coaching or mentoring sessions. I have to admit I found the experience quite draining at first.

It must have been a concern that the technology might let me down, or that my usual line of patter – well tested in a live situation – wouldn't go across on the small screen; but I would end each session feeling like a wrung out dish rag, or feeling like I had just given blood!

And then I realised what was missing was feedback from the audience, all that lovely affirmation, the nods and smiles of encouragement you get from a training room or conference audience, that returns your energy to you in spades. It is there online too, but you have to work for it, and it is definitely harder to pick up on a screen full of thumbnail pictures.

Transitioning online brought home very clearly to

me one of the main points of all communication - that it is always a two-way street. Even where you are the presenter or lecturer or main speaker, you have to engage your audience and get them to work with you, or your words will fall on deaf ears.

In this chapter we will explore all the ways in which you can develop screen presence and really connect with your audience, so that you can present, contribute and interview really well online. In later chapters, we go into live communication in detail, as we return to in-person events and we see conferences, town halls and team events get fully underway once more.

Show Your Face!

Have you ever listened to a disembodied voice on a webinar, hiding behind multiple slides, droning on and on, and felt that life was really, really too short for this? You probably let it run in the background, and went off to make tea, and no one blames you.

Don't be that voice!

We like the human face and learn to read it from infancy. Yours is a very fine face indeed, and one we need to see clearly when you start presenting so we can get to know you a little, and get a sense of your enthusiasm and knowledge. Long before we get to the detail, the 'how' of what you are saying, we need to understand the 'why' - that is, why we should listen to you. And your lovely face will tell us that better than anything else.

So show yourself at the start in full screen, make a connection, win us over, catch our attention, and then if you have to, you can share your screen later to show illustrations. A bit like the news presenter who introduces the story, then shows us the news reel, and comes back to us at the end of it to give us a back reference before going on to introduce the next story.

You can also learn from the newscaster about positioning your face in the screen. Your eyes should be about one third down from the top, and you achieve this by placing the laptop on top of a few books, until you get it to the right height. And then place a lamp behind the laptop to light your face, and show it clearly to your appreciative audience.

Whatever you do, don't have the camera shooting up your nose and don't have the ceiling tilting behind you, making the viewer uneasy.

Do you know where the camera on your screen is situated? Put a little red sticker beside it to remind yourself to look at it! You don't have to lock on to it constantly, but you should be directing your presentation at it where possible, naturally breaking contact from time to time to glance at notes, or to look away, as we do in normal conversation.

The Background

I mentioned the universities digital project earlier in the introduction. At first, when the lecturers did get online, they did not insist that students were in vision, aware that some might be self-conscious about less than tidy accommodation, with beer bottles or a clothes horse in the background. The faculty sensitivity is admirable, but as a presenter or contributor to an online event, you need to get the background sorted so that you are comfortable being in vision as often as you can.

A tidy bookshelf in the background works well,

or a plain wall with a couple of bland pictures. Try not to let the bedposts show on screen, or the kettle and microwave. Most platforms now have a blur feature which you can use, and some have a green screen where you can add your own background picture.

I have a few backgrounds loaded on my laptop which I alternate between, one is my living room photographed on a day when I could clear the furniture and make sure it was empty of dogs and lounging bodies.

Neat and professional is the look we are going for, and the same with the clothes we choose for an important online event, with simple necklines and block colours probably best.

Sounds, Distractions and Technology

At the start of the mass transition online, I think we were all very tolerant of couriers arriving at the kitchen door, cats sitting on the keyboard and children crying in the middle of a meeting. We are probably less so today, as we figure people should have all of this stuff worked out by now.

If these things do happen in the middle of your interview or presentation, try to do a Bryan on it and remain unflustered and undistracted. But the main thing is to minimise the chances of interruptions before you start.

You do this by having a partner or family member on stand-by, if possible, to deal with the household stuff for the time you are online. Silence your phone before you start, turn off all pings or notifications on the laptop, turn off any machinery that might hum, and put a large "silence" notice on the outside of the door, in case someone suddenly decides now is a good time to vacuum the landing.

You can of course mitigate against normal household sounds to some extent by investing in a good headset with a built-in microphone that cancels or neutralizes outside sounds, and allows your voice to be picked up as clearly as possible.

Check your equipment thoroughly to be absolutely confident your microphone, webcam and wi-fi are working properly on the day. Close down all the tabs on your computer except the ones you will be using. You don't want to share something inappropriate by accident, or to have band-width used up unnecessarily, causing your presentation to drop out. And make sure there are no updates running in the background.

Practise your presentation out loud going from in-vision to slide share and back to in-vision again. You should be able to do this smoothly without losing your train of thought or fumbling about too much. And practice muting and unmuting yourself – the appropriate buttons are in different places depending on the platform you are using.

And you know during the live presentation, if things don't work in the moment for any reason, just smile, keep talking, and try again. Think of the newscaster who smiles and says, "We seem to be having a technical difficulty with that report, we'll come back to it in a moment, in the meantime ..."

And they go right on to the next story without batting an eyelid.

It reminds me of a conference where the power dropped out in the entire locality because a construction worker outside had dug up a mains cable by mistake. The man whose turn it was to speak, could have blacked out himself! His microphone was dead, his PowerPoint was dead, his video content was gone, but you know what? He didn't die.

He picked up a sheet of paper, shaped it into a cone, put it to his mouth like a megaphone and said, "It must have been like this during the war. Can you all hear me down the back? Yes? Do I even need this thing? No? Well, let's continue at this volume and I'll tell you some stories and we'll see how we get on. I probably had way too many slides anyway." He won the crowd over and everyone loved him.

In the Mood

The activist and poet Maya Angelou famously said "People will forget what you said, people will forget what you did, but people will never forget how you made them feel." So in an online presentation, your tone of voice is nearly as important as what you are saying, because that is what makes your audience warm to you from the get go, and feel good about you.

Remember what we said about the droney voiced webinar, and the overwhelming switch-off impulse it creates? If you sound happy, enthusiastic and up-beat, your audience will absolutely want to hear more.

So put yourself in a good mood before you start. Get out into the fresh air, walk the dog, go for a run, do a few stretches – whatever works for you to get the blood pumping and takes you into a happy, confident, bring-it-on zone.

Unfortunately we, the audience, judge a

presentation very quickly. As in, within the first thirty seconds. So your voice, your tone, your eye contact, your smile, your overall look are measured right from the start, which takes us nicely to your opening salvo.

The Opening

In Chapter Three of this book, which covers presenting and public speaking in detail, I talk about the Big Opening - that story or really interesting statement or question a good speaker always uses as a hook, to reel us in from the very start. It is no different online, you should start your contribution with something that makes us turn up the volume on our device, and lean right in to hear more.

It's too easy to start with my name is such and such and I have been asked here today to talk to you...

So far, so ordinary. No reason yet for me to turn up the volume, because I probably already knew your name and why you were there. So I might actually wander off to put on the kettle at this point, and you have lost some of your audience before you ever got going.

Start with something I don't know. Jump right in with an interesting statement or quotation, a story or example, a surprising fact or statistic - something that gets me thinking, and in other words gets me engaging from the very start. The coffee can wait.

Next, go straight to the biggest thing your talk or presentation has to offer. Give away the best bit right now, don't make people wait to till the end. In a live presentation, we often build up to a reveal, or a discovery or a give-away or prize. We can't do that online, as time online has a completely different quality, and we have to cut to the chase to hold people in.

Moving Along

I have suggested you drop in and out of a slide presentation, using your face and eye contact as often as possible to win people over. Visuals are very helpful when used sparingly and correctly, not as something to hide behind. In Chapter Two I deal with the dreaded *Death by PowerPoint,* where a presenter overloads us with word heavy slides we cannot possibly take on board, and loses both us and themselves in the process.

Remember the reason for a slide in the first place is to show something that you can't really explain; to re-enforce a message and help us remember it; to add variety and interest, or to make us smile! A slide should never be your script and should have the absolute minimum of words on it.

People often ask for a copy of the slides after a presentation, clearly coming from a corporate background where the slides, no matter what best practice tells us, *are* the script. Deal with that by having a fact sheet to share after the presentation, so that you don't destroy the opportunity of a live encounter by locking yourself into a bad slide deck.

Making the Audience Work

An online audience that is listening passively is not working, and is therefore only taking in a fraction of what you are saying. An audience that is actively thinking, engaging and mentally questioning is working, and is therefore taking in most if not all of what you are saying. So how to make them work? Set them up to work before you start!

Describe your event as a 'camera-on, interactive workshop' and people will dress to be in vision and prepare to take part. Otherwise an invitation might sound like a webinar, where it's too easy to leave the camera off and let it play in the background without really engaging. It is so much harder to present to a screen full of avatars, than it is to present to a row of real live faces.

A chatty style with plenty of rhetorical questions sounds like a conversation, and the audience responds accordingly. Look at the thumbnails on the screen if the gallery feature is in use, you will see people nodding, smiling and clearly going along with you. Contrast that to when a speaker reads a script, sounds overly formal, or uses a flat tone of voice, the faces on the screen will be disengaged, rooting around at things on their own desks, or you will see empty chairs, as people wander off to do something else.

Ask for a show of hands. Pose a relevant question, and ask the audience to raise their hand if they agree. Look at the gallery and guesstimate the result. "So that is about 30% of you who agree, I'd love to know why the rest of you don't agree, maybe you would put your thoughts into the chat box and I'll read some of them out at the end".

Use a quiz or poll feature. Have a few relevant questions prepared before-hand, ask people to answer the questions, give them a minute or two to take part, and again you can reveal the results at the end.

Use the rooms feature where appropriate. Tell the group you are going to drop them into rooms of a few people for several minutes and give them a topic to discuss.

After five minutes you will be bringing them back into the round, and you will ask one person to speak on behalf of the group to share what was discussed.

Tell the audience, after your presentation is underway, that you will be happy to take questions, and that they can pop them into the chat box. Experienced presenters often take these questions on the fly, and seamlessly build them in to the content of their presentation. Don't worry if that is a step too far for you at this point, you can easily come to the questions at the end.

Body Language

Your audience can't see as much of you as they would if you were standing at the top of the room. Even so, they can see enough of you to judge, by your expressions, how concerned you are about your issue and how comfortable you are to be presenting on it.

Positive facial expressions are really important. So we need to work on looking happy, relaxed, enthusiastic, and really interested in reaching the audience with this important message.

Sit up straight in your chair, with your back well supported so you are not leaning too far forward or too far back. Use a solid chair rather than a swivel chair if possible so that you don't move about inadvertently and so the wheels don't squeak. Any movements you do make should be expressive, deliberate and in sync with what you are saying.

Some presenters deliberately move back from the camera to allow more of their body and their hand gestures to be seen, believing that a hands-out open palms stance looks welcoming. And yes it does, but by doing this you risk losing some sound quality, unless you are wearing a tie-pin mic. More about that further on, in the section on key-note speaking.

Hand gestures are completely normal, and usually indicate a presenter who is in the moment, and really working to make sure what they are saying is interesting. A note of caution – make sure your hand gestures don't cross in front of the screen like wind screen wipers, which could be very distracting.

Ending Well

How you end your online presentation is as important as how you start it. No one enjoys a presentation that runs out of energy, like a balloon losing air and floating listlessly to the ground. End decisively with a vision of how things can be, with a call to action, with a relevant story or anecdote or by remembering to ask for the job or the sale.

You can then take questions, if that is how the event is structured.

Where you feel there won't be time for questions, or where that is not the format, just before you come to your ending, after your last major point has been made, include a few comments from the chat box, respond to any queries, thank people for their participation and go to your prepared ending with a flourish. This ends your contribution by drawing a definitive line under it, rather than by fizzling out.

Interviewing online

Notwithstanding all of the above, which applies to every online engagement, there are a few specifics to note for an online job interview, which we will deal with here. Chapter Three covers the full preparation required for getting the perfect job.

Online job interviews are often a preliminary chat, a weeding out of the large numbers who have applied for the role, to decide who to take forward to the next round, which may well be in person. You are aiming to come across as qualified for the role, competent, and confident.

Arrive early! If the online meeting is planned for 2 pm, be there online, composed and ready to go, by five minutes to two at the latest, with a glass of water beside you and a notebook and pen ready in case you want to jot things down. Try not to use a phone or small device, if possible, or to use your computer on your lap. Have the device firmly placed on a desk, so you can attend to the eye levels, background, noise and lighting mentioned before.

Dress appropriately, and make sure you feel smart and comfortable, which will add to your confidence levels.

Remember the little red sticker beside the camera? This is where you need to look when you are speaking and particularly when the interviewer is speaking. Use the mute button while she is asking you her questions, or telling you a bit about the company, to keep your household sounds distraction to a minimum.

Keep a strong focus while the interviewer is speaking, actively listening, nodding and giving affirmation, and looking out for two part or three part questions.

Signal how you are going to answer to affirm you have heard correctly. "I'll take the question about my education first and then move on to the second part about my last job, if that is ok".

Have a few questions prepared, so you can ask them when the time is right. Things like:

- What do people say is the best thing about working with your company?

- How would you describe the company culture?

- What is the reporting structure in this role?

- How do people generally progress within the company?

- Can you tell me a little bit more about the day to day responsibilities of the role?

A few good pre-prepared questions show that you are thinking seriously about the position, and avoid the awkwardness of giving a flat 'no' when asked at the end have you any questions, or anything to say.

Contributing to an Online Meeting

A recent coachee of mine was promoted to general manager, and was attending the national online meeting of Group GMs for the first time. She was very anxious about how her first report would land, in front of a very experienced group of peers. However, the CEO had also changed at this time, and the new CEO shook everyone up by saying he was not going around the houses getting a report from everyone anymore, it was a complete waste of time. He would only want to hear from people who had something useful to say.

My client had her online wave hand up before she knew what she was doing, and gave a short pithy and really insightful report. Afterwards she was thrilled that she had spoken at all, that she had jumped in without any thought, that she had delivered her message well, and most of all that she got great compliments afterwards.

The trick was in the preparation. We had prepared a short contribution that was all about insight, not so much about information. The problem with a round the houses reporting structure is that people feel compelled to fill you in on every single thing they have done since you last met, rather than giving a good example of how something is working on the front line, or sharing some experience that others can learn from.

Read the meeting agenda and decide where you are going to contribute and how you are going to contribute. Tell them something they don't already know, give them something to think about, share information that you are hearing, ask for insights from others present – in other words, make your contribution useful and memorable, rather than rote.

It is not the person who talks most at an online meeting that stands out, it is often the person who brings something interesting and different to the airwaves.

Chairing an Online Meeting

Chapter Six covers in some detail the factors that make a good general meeting chair. The main difference for online chairmanship is the awareness that concentration spans are shorter, the time can feel longer, signal dropouts can make organisation of people and contributions difficult, and interruptions or speaking over one another can be lethal.

The CEO mentioned above, who changed the format of his monthly GMs meeting, is to be hugely commended. Can you just imagine how tedious it must have been to have to listen to 20 people give a repetitive, boring update online? And can you also imagine how everyone zoned out as people were speaking, ignoring what was going on until it came to their own turn to speak?

As an online meeting organiser or chair, your job is all about timing, tone and tempo. People's time is valuable. Respect it by starting and finishing on time, and giving the right amount of time to each agenda item. Keep the tone light and interesting. It doesn't matter how formal or serious the subject matter might be, we look forward to a meeting where the tone is amenable and pleasant, we dread a meeting that is stiff and stilted.

And keep the pace moving along nicely. The best chairs allow people to feel they were given time, and not rushed, yet the meeting moves along and doesn't run over. The best chairs build a reputation for running a good meeting.

As a meeting organiser, here is your "to do" list:

1. Tell people what time the meeting will finish, as well as what time it will start

2.   Make sure everyone has access to the platform chosen

3.   Issue an agenda, and if that sounds too formal, a few points that are to be covered

4.   Make sure attendees know what is expected of them by way of contribution to each item. Discussion? Decision? Brain storm? Report?

5.   Start on time, a bit of catch-up chat for a minute or two is nice, if appropriate

6.   Outline a framework, what is going to happen, what are the outcomes hoped for, how people should contribute. Welcome any late arrivals

7.   Declare the meeting open and get underway

8.   Introduce the first item

9.   Call people in to speak, and look out for hands raised

10. Watch your screen gallery and note how engaged people are

11. Refer to people by name from time to time to keep them focused

12. Sum up each item, thanking the contributor and repeating the decision made or the way forward

13. Keep it light-hearted and interesting and move on smoothly from one item to the next

14. Five minutes before the end begin to wrap up, finish on time, thank participants, and agree on next meeting.

A Keynote Speech Online

I mentioned earlier that some presenters like to move back from the screen to use positive body language to full advantage. When the world closed down and everything went online overnight, including large conferences, many regular speakers I know purchased all kinds of kit as fast as they could, so they could stand, move about and deliver their speech looking and behaving as they normally would.

They had backdrops designed to stand in front of, and tie-pin mics on a long lead attached to the computer, or a blue-tooth head set linked up, so they could stand well back and the quality of voice would not be lost.

And indeed so the presenter would not sound as if they were speaking from the bathroom!

Then came the positioning of the laptop or iPad, with stands employed to get the device to the perfect height. And professional lighting, in the hope of really reaching across the miles to those on line and those few at the event, if it was hybrid.

I'm not sure all of this achieved a whole lot, to be honest. At the first post-mayhem conference I went to, featuring both in-person and online presenters, the outstanding online speeches in the auditorium were those where the presenter appeared in big close-up, like a newscaster. Back to that again!

Those who were standing back appeared a bit removed to me, and probably made things difficult for anyone watching on a smart phone, whereas those well lit, in full screen, giving us the benefit of all their facial expressions, eye rolls and shoulder shrugs really stood out.

It seems to me that connection as an online keynote speaker is far more about the relevance of your topic to the audience, how much you hold and entertain them, and how well you use your voice and intonation, rather than trying to add movement and a full body position on a screen that is the wrong shape in the first place.

Think about it, most screens are horizontal. So shoot that way for professional situations. Only use your phone to shoot vertically when you are intending the material to be viewed on a platform such as TikTok.

Slides need to be kept to a complete minimum.

Think about the audience in the auditorium in a hybrid event. You are this interesting person who has dropped in from abroad to join them and share your wisdom. Make sure you have really connected with them by using a good introductory hook, and a great set-up of your premise, before you disappear behind a few slides.

And make sure to pop back on screen several times throughout, to keep the connection going, and to pose rhetorical questions to encourage a conversational tone, such as:

How's that sounding so far?

You are probably wondering how this will impact on you? … Let me tell you.

Have you ever thought about what would happen if? …. I think it could look like this.

Come back into vision at the end to wrap up and go to your prepared strong ending.

—◆◇◆—

Online communication is here to stay. From now on it will be seamlessly woven into all we do, and will be part and parcel of every educational course, onboarding experience, and day to day workload. That we all have to get comfortable with it, and learn to use it as well as we can, is a given.

I hope the ideas here have given you something to think about, and some techniques to try out from the comfort of your home. The following chapters delve much further into talks, presentations and other forms of in-person workplace communication. You'll find lots of clear structures and ideas to help you prepare for them, so you can really develop your personal skills and career.

Chapter Two

The Communications Audit

In this chapter we take a look at our personal communication, and delve into the things that make us look and sound competent and in control. We also consider what prevents us from taking the opportunity to step up and shine, and we analyse and deal with nervousness.

When the memoir of the late and much admired RTE journalist Nuala O'Faolain was published some years back, I remember thinking that the title she had chosen, *Are You Somebody?* was a little bit of magic. With searing honesty, she shared enormous doubts about her own contribution to the world, despite having been a very successful columnist and radio producer.

Her book was a runaway bestseller, touching a chord with people all over the world who felt as she did and, I am sure, hugely appreciated the honesty of a public figure baring all.

Nuala's doubts are shared by most of us if we are honest enough to admit it. No matter how well we craft our front, our outward face, there are times when we feel alone and struggling and we wonder if we are making any kind of difference at all.

But we know that the best learning is done on the edge; in that place where you feel the fear and do it anyway. Becoming a really effective communicator in the workplace context is all about pushing your limits; putting your hand up and offering to give the speech, make the pitch or lead the negotiation, the very action that might result in failure, or great success.

Working with a group of senior female managers in a bank, we were discussing performance at the front-line, and I was challenging them to honestly assess their personal performance on different bases.

One manager said that she sometimes had trouble stating clearly where she stood on a particular issue. She said she was inclined to wait and see how others were thinking before revealing her position. She was concerned that this was making her appear weak, or uncertain.

The other managers then chimed in that they too had stayed quiet, on occasion, when they should have owned their positions confidently and clearly.

We did some exercises around firstly working out what your position actually is, and secondly how to contribute in a way that will be impactful, and will persuade others to your way of thinking, techniques that are covered in the chapter on meetings.

Meetings, presentations, negotiations and pitches are the front line – the place where you have to put up or push off. Two more bases of extreme importance are the way you show up as a coach, and how you play out on the media. To my mind, these skills are vital, and the good news is that they are infinitely learnable and applicable – once you get over the know-do gap.

In *The Knowing-Doing Gap*, Jeffrey Pfeffer and Robert I. Sutton provide a great description of the organisational paralysis that sees eye-wateringly large sums spent on consultants, and then not a single recommendation implemented.

They talk about the months and years of person hours spent on strategy summits and organisational realignments, complete with slide decks and fancy bound planning documents – the perpetrators thinking that all the talking and report writing constitutes real action.

We did a report and there were lots of findings. How often have you heard that?

But those people are actually crippled by fear. Any action risks failure, so the best thing to do is to put the report on the shelf and not actually do anything. If you do, you risk censure, the criticism of colleagues, loss of face, loss of position.

The opportunity to develop and communicate best practice across an organisation is completely lost in a cloud of fear, and a cloud of individual reluctance to stand up and be counted.

But the fact that you are reading this suggests that you want to be different, that you want to check in on your skill sets in these areas to see if you have kept up to speed. Learning is layered, as you well know, and we all have to keep adding to it to keep it fresh.

And if you are at an early stage in your career, it is terrific that you are thinking about these things already. Practice certainly does make perfect, and getting performance miles on your clock is what it is all about.

In doing a personal performance audit across the bases mentioned we have to consider how we show up;

how alive, present, engaged, mindful, in the moment we are on a day-to-day basis.

How prepared are we? How do we deliver? How do others rate us? How do we translate all our management learning and university study into practical performance at the front line?

If you find that your communication is less than you would want, is it your fault or that of your organisation? Definitely, there are organisations which seem to suck the life out of individuals; which lack the ability to take the collective knowledge of its people and turn it into positive action.

But there are also lots of organisations who manage to get great results out of very ordinary people, usually by having a strong learning culture, and by using the oldest training method in the book – *hear one, see one, do one.* So you read about or study a great presentation or pitch, then you go and watch one, and then you do one yourself.

Ultimately we are all fully responsible for our own communication. If I give a pitch to a client, and it falls flat, I can't go back to the office complaining that 'they didn't get us' or 'they didn't understand the concepts'. If they didn't understand every word I was saying, it is 100 per cent my fault. The responsibility to make them understand lies with me, not with them.

The Dreaded Nerves

So what is holding you back from front line performance? From putting yourself forward to do the media interview, or take on the keynote speech? Is it perhaps anxiety? A concern about how you will look and sound in front of colleagues, how you will acquit yourself, how you will deal with the pressure of the moment and the rows of faces looking up at you expectantly?

Everybody gets nervous before a major event, even the most experienced of public performers. If they tell you they are not nervous, they are lying! They are definitely feeling the impact of the adrenaline rush, but what they have learned to do is to channel it in the right direction, and to use it as fuel.

Mastering nerves is the art of first understanding the symptoms, then minimising them, and then developing a system to turn them into performance energy.

Ronan O'Gara, rugby fly-half for both Ireland and Munster for many years, had the most outstanding focus every time he took a penalty kick. You could see the intense concentration on his face as he placed the ball, went through a set pattern of steps, and took his shot with unbelievable accuracy. You knew that a bomb could go off in the stadium at the same time, and he wouldn't hear it.

He was in a state of Flow, as described by psychologist Mihaly Csikszentmihalyi: "A sense that one's skills are adequate to cope with the challenges at hand, in a goal-directed, rule-bound action system that provides clear clues as to how well one is performing".

Flow is that state of intense happiness that comes about when you are on a roll, you have done the prep, you are up to the task, it all goes to plan, and you are delivering the performance of your life. It is a high – almost a euphoric state – an optimal experience.

It comes about as a result of using systems, building skills, focusing intently, cutting out distractions, and quantifying results.

The systems are what this book is about, straightforward steps towards building the skills that will allow you to perform to a higher level than ever before. And it will show you how and where to focus, so the distractions are eliminated.

Hopefully, you will start to get the results you need, and will be encouraged by those results to stay on this journey of achieving excellence in communication.

So let's start by looking at the physical symptoms of nervousness, the things that hit you in that moment when you go up on stage, or stand up in the boardroom to make the most important pitch of your career. Most people say they experience a selection of the following in the moments before they are due to start:

- Shaking hands
- Tapping Feet
- Dry mouth
- Butterflies in the tummy
- Faster heart beat
- Perspiration
- Distorted hearing
- Distorted vision

They are all caused by the same thing – the fight or flight drug, adrenaline. It is an evolutionary adaptation to allow the body to react quickly to danger; the hypothalamus instantly signalling the adrenal glands to release adrenaline into the blood stream, causing blood vessels to contract in the extremities, redirecting the blood to the heart and lungs to increase physical performance.

Have you ever bent to pet a friend's sweet-looking dog, and nearly jumped out of your skin when it suddenly snapped at you? The hairs on the back of your neck stand up as the adrenaline floods your body in a nanosecond. It is unbelievably fast and equally powerful.

Athletes often call it the 119 per cent drug because strength and speed increase, while the body's ability to feel pain decreases, allowing those phenomenal performances to be pulled out of the bag on the day of a big event.

The problem with boardroom or public speaking performance is that our bodies are preparing for physical danger, sometimes from the day before! They don't realise that we are not being threatened by wild animals or a marauding army. The threat is psychological, and not physical – the psychological threat of failure, shame, reputational damage, or criticism.

In the boardroom, we don't actually need our hearts pumping twice as fast as normal, and our lungs gobbling up air like it was going out of fashion.

But if we learn to welcome the adrenaline rush as an asset, an ally there to help us, it becomes easier to control.

So, on the morning of the big event, you wake up with that feeling in your stomach, and the racing effect beginning. Before you even get out of the bed do these things:

1. Remind yourself that this is the cavalry riding over the hill to help you. Tell yourself this is good. Really good. If you listen hard enough, you will even hear the bugles!

2.   Now remind yourself of the preparation you have done for the event. You have the best possible material gathered, a great structure worked out, and you know exactly where you are going with the message.

3.   Now focus on the task ahead – delivering the message to the audience in a way that they will really relate to, understand and buy into.

4.   Imagine the end result, your objectives achieved. Hold the thought, and get on with your day.

You will be hard put to find a better definition of nervousness than this: Nervousness is the moment when we focus on our *ability* to do the task, and forget to focus on *the task itself.*

The trick with all performance is to mentally turn the spotlight in the other direction, and to make the communication all about the audience and their needs, not about yourself.

On the other hand if we allow the emotional response of the adrenaline rush to be one of panic, and we don't mentally manage it and acknowledge it, guess what happens? Our bodies decide that we didn't get enough adrenaline the first time, and very helpfully send us another shot, the second dose strong enough to fell an elephant!

This can result in light-headedness, dizziness and actual changes in vision, the effect lasting for up to an hour.

And you were thinking of performing with all of that going on?

So the key to the emotional management of adrenaline, before we get to the physical management, is to welcome it and to remind yourself to stay task and result focused – not to get bogged down in negative thoughts like:

- 'Am I good enough for this task?'
- 'Should someone else be doing it?'
- 'I'm bound to screw up.'
- 'Will they like me?'
- 'My accent is hard to understand.'
- 'I wish I didn't use so many ums and ahs.'
- 'The sales manager is out to get me.'
- 'I wish I didn't have a spot on my chin.'

All of these thoughts turn the giant imaginary spotlight inward, and can destroy a performance by altering the whole focus of the presentation or communication. The physical symptoms of the adrenaline rush are very manageable too – once we know why they are happening, and once we learn to use adrenaline as it is supposed to be used, to help us and not to hinder us.

Shaking Hands: The rush of blood to the vital organs, to help with slaying potential dragons, leaves our extremities deprived. Have you ever cringed as a nervous colleague stumbles with the mouse, and goes five slides forward, then three back, stuttering and apologising and getting redder and redder in the face?

The poor thing doesn't realise that his fingers are slightly numb. He knows how to use a mouse – he uses

41

one every day – he just can't feel it properly this day, because of the pressure of the occasion.

Before you start a big presentation, you have to physically tell your brain that your hands are still working – 'It's fine, I understand this stuff, I definitely do not need more adrenaline, thank you.' Before every important speech, Bill Clinton used to dig the thumbnail of one hand into the palm of the other, and then reverse it, to tell his brain that his hands were fine, and to instantly remove any suggestion of a shake.

On a stage, the last thing you want to see is shaking hands, or the opposite, a white knuckled death grip on either side of the podium.

Tapping Feet: At the start of a race, before the runners get down to the blocks, what are they doing? The are jumping around, slapping their sides, doing kicks and hops and mini sprints – physically telling the brain that the extremities are in good working order and that they haven't gone away.

In the same way, experienced speakers will be pacing in the green room before the conference, walking up and down to focus their thoughts and manage their brain/feet messaging.

At the podium, feet that haven't first been reconnected with the brain will respond to regular check-in signals by making you tick-tock from side to side, or lean forward and back, both of which make you look shifty, and far less credible.

Some of the most comfortable speakers in the world abandon the podium altogether, and use movement to help hold on to the audience. But more about that later.

Dry Mouth: Is your mouth really dry, or does it just feel like that? Remember the hairs on the back of the neck in the driving incident? Your neck and throat area are highly sensitised in an adrenaline rush, because they are very important areas to protect during fight or flight.

You are really aware of them now, in a way that you are not usually. So the normal, regular re-salivation you do during conversation hundreds of times a day now becomes 'clicky' and noticeable.

The trick is to hydrate well before the speech or presentation, and it will be less of a problem. Sip water in the green room for a while before the event, not coffee or cola.

Butterflies in the Tummy: You know the feeling, the stomach fluttering and churning causing an unpleasant discomfort and for many, a scramble around the desk drawers for the antacids.

What has happened is that the digestive tract has had some of its normal blood supply diverted to the heart, and the digestive acids are left to have a field day, gnawing away at the lining of your stomach. The coffees and the colas before the event make this much worse.

I find it very hard to eat properly before a big event, so I go for something light and protein based – scrambled eggs or yoghurt are good for me – but it is important to find something that works for you and settles you down.

Faster Heartbeat: The blood that has left your stomach has gone straight to your heart and, as the entire body is over sensitised, you can hear it loudly and clearly. Imagine if you could hear your heart like that all the time. You would never get any work done, or get any sleep.

No one else can hear it, but the racket it is making is seriously distracting, and is making it so hard to do as I have suggested above, to focus on the audience and the message and not the self.

Every part of this adrenaline rush is screaming at you to focus on the self. But maybe now that you know what is happening, and why it is happening, it might be a bit easier to control.

Perspiration: So you are in the middle of the talk, and you suddenly realise you have a bead of perspiration running down your side, tracking its way from rib to rib, under your shirt, to land who knows where. The big spotlight has just been taken away from the audience again, and turned back on to the self.

But here is the thing. No one else actually knows about that rogue bead of sweat. In fact, it is probably there every day of the week, particularly during the summer months, unnoticed, getting on with its job of cooling you down.

In your adrenaline induced heightened sensitivity moment, you feel it, you notice it, and you start confusing your brain by thinking about it. Forget it, get on with the talk.

Distorted Hearing: This is the 'bomb going off in the stadium and the player hearing nothing' moment. That dulling of external, unnecessary noise, and the ability to focus on the moment, is the source of 'Flow'.

Used correctly it is a huge asset. Misunderstood, or used incorrectly, it is a source of sheer panic and yes, you guessed it, a signal to the body to land in more adrenaline, the second dose the one that makes think you are actually going to collapse.

Distorted Vision: It is sometimes called 'threat locking', that sensation where the rows of faces blur in front of you, but you can see as clear as day the person in row 13 who you think dislikes you, or who is your main competitor.

Internalised, this moment becomes all about you and your ability to perform. Externalised, this sharp focus is what makes Ronan O'Gara hit his target, and what can make you really see and feel what it is your audience wants and needs, right at this moment, to make this whole experience for them, and for you, get into 'flow'.

How To Fix Nervousness

There are many other symptoms of nervousness and adrenaline-rush aside from the ones described here, and they each have a very good physiological reason for occurring. The good news is that once they are understood, they can be dealt with, and the energy generated used as a force for achievement.

So we 'fix' nervousness firstly by preparing in advance for our known and usual physical manifestations of it, and secondly by giving our brain tasks during the performance to keep it externally focused.

Unfortunately, during many of our key performances – pitching for a really important piece of business, making a significant speech, presenting to a room full of colleagues and peers – we do not trust our brains, so we give them far too little to do, and they begin to work against us.

Here is what happens.

Earlier I described the 119 per cent state in which you are operating at this crucial time, assisted by the wonder drug, adrenaline. Your brain is as sharp, focused, and geared up for action as it has ever been in its entire life. And what do you do? You decide to use the great big idiot board known as power point, where the only thing your brain has to do is to read from slides, using up maybe 20 per cent of capacity.

What happens to all the spare capacity? Your brain now becomes your worst critic, starting a running commentary on how badly you are presenting, how poorly the audience is reacting, how badly prepared your slides are, and horror of horrors, is that a typo I have just spotted?

During a slide presentation, this often happens:

What the Presenter says:	What you think:
'I'm not sure if you can see this graph'	*Of course I can't at the back of the hall!*
'I'll just skip a few slides'	*So why are they there in the first place?*
'You may not be interested in this	*You think?*
'You'll see from the bullet points here.'	*No I can't, I don't have bionic sight!*
'And the bullet points here'	*You mean there's more of them?*
'There is probably too much detail'	*So why the hell is it there!!*
'I'm not sure what I was going to say about this slide'	*You've lost yourself now, and you've definitely lost me.*

This, tragically, is a presenter becoming deeply self-conscious about his own presentation, and worse still, chronically unhappy with it – his own brain beginning to campaign against him, because he just did not give it enough to do.

And at this point, when he realises that he has locked himself into a relentlessly rigid format, where slide 13 has to come after slide 12, and slide 28, sadly and tragically, has to come after slide 27, he begins to crumble in front of our eyes. He has no way out, and no means of getting back to what the audience wants or needs.

This is truly Death by PowerPoint.

The alternative is to trust your brilliant, fantastic and enormous brain to do the job it was designed to do, particularly when your system is full of adrenaline. You set it tasks to focus on, tasks that are all about delivering a presentation that is audience rather than self-focussed and you achieve them by working from the correct part of your memory.

Learned Versus Personal Memory

The linear presentation described above will be flat, dull and boring for a lot of reasons, not least because the presenter can't possibly show or produce the best part of himself in that format. Even those who are completely comfortable with slide presentations, and who don't get fussed up or bothered by nerves, will completely close off their communication.

The reason is that learned memory is like a drawer in a filing cabinet, with the information stored in a certain order. And we can only access the information in the same order in which we stored it in the first place.

So if you remember when you were at school, and asked by the teacher to recite, you stood up at your desk and began your poem, this one by Robert Herrick:

> *'Fair Daffodils we weep to see*
> *You haste away so soon*
> *As yet the early-rising sun…'*

And then you got the brain freeze and said: 'Sorry Teacher, I'll have to start again', and this time you take a really good run at it and get a bit further.

> 'Fair Daffodils we weep to see
> You haste away so soon
> As yet the early-rising sun
> Has not attain'd his noon.
> Stay, stay until the hasting day
> Has run to the even-song
> And having pray'd together,
> We will go with you along.'

It only works if you take it all together at a run. Don't ask me to pick a word in the middle, and try to start reciting from there. My brain can only access the verse in sequential order.

The other interesting thing about learned memory is how I can't possibly make eye contact with you while I am accessing it. As I pause and go looking for the words, my eyes will go off up to the sky, as if it is from there I have to pull the information down.

When I get the information, I can only deliver it in a sing-song, obviously recited tone of voice, and if I lose my place, I am completely goosed, and may well freeze and completely embarrass myself.

So the sequential format of a slide deck, even where we are really accomplished presenters, locks us into learned memory, information that we can only deliver in a rote way, which makes us stilted and formal, and reduces the chance of any fluency, fluidity or any interactivity with the audience.

Add to that the 'theatre effect' of a formal presentation – the audience sitting back and expecting a show, becoming passive and non-responsive – and you are really making your work difficult for yourself.

In fact using learned memory takes up so much of our concentration, that we sometimes shut out that pesky audience altogether, and focus completely on reciting facts and figures, without any reference to relevance, or to the capacity of the audience to take any of it in.

Using predominantly learned memory formalises our language, and our whole demeanour, body language and appearance, and drops us down to the very bottom rung of the communications ladder. This is the one that loudly tells the audience that now is a great time to zone out and start thinking about what they will have for dinner.

Certainly, reciting a few lines of a verse is a device that can be used very well in a presentation, as long it is clearly flagged as a pause for thought.

But a whole presentation that relies on learned memory is doomed to failure. It will fail because it puts the presenter in the wrong place, it puts the audience in the wrong place, and it puts the messaging in the wrong place.

Personal memory, on the other hand, makes our communication come alive; it's the part of our brain and memory usage that shows our personality and it clearly gives the audience the 'why' they should listen to our message, long before we expect them to follow the nuts and bolts of the 'how'.

Personal memory is all about our personality, knowledge, insights, and understanding; the things the audience actually came out to hear.

We never lose our place or get stuck in personal memory and we never lock out the audience. We use conversational every-day language when we are in personal memory, we use colour and description, we tell stories and hold the attention, and we bring our communication right up to the highest rung of the ladder.

Personal memory is that moment when someone who has been giving a fairly dry talk, or reading tonelessly from something prepared, suddenly puts down the script and says: 'You know, what I really want to say to you today is….'

And just watch the room go silent, and the eyes come up from the phones.

We all know something good is coming and we pay attention.

The great Irish actor Eamon Kelly understood that the role of the story teller or *Seanchaí* was to keep people enthralled, and to bring people real news – in those days long before the internet or even TV or radio. All his stories came straight from personal memory, keeping them lively and in the moment.

In one scenario, the *Seanchaí* is drawing a map of New York on the hearth of the cottage in which he is sitting, using the ashes from the fire and a poker. An early version of the flip chart, you could say.

And as he explains where cousin John is living now, and where Betty's son Paul is headed, to a rapt audience, a cat leaps into the middle of the picture, scattering the Bronx and Staten Island all the way to New Jersey.

The simple story and dramatic effect has relevance, urgency, unpredictability.

The art of good communication is giving a series of

those moments, and having the confidence to reveal the authentic self while doing do.

In performance audit terms, these are the questions we have to ask ourselves about how we have been showing up in the past, and how we are going to do it differently in the future.

- Are we really reaching the audience every time we speak?

- Are the meetings we attend productive and effective?

- When it is our turn to chair, are we doing it effectively and efficiently?

- Are we using coaching conversations where possible?

- Are we pitching the project, the idea or the business in a way that will connect with the manager or potential investor?

- Are we comfortable taking media opportunities?

—⚡—

In the next few chapters, I will show you exactly how you can up your game in all of these areas so you can always communicate well in the workplace.

Chapter Three

Get That Job

There are lots of jobs out there - in your existing company, in a brand new one, or in the one you have targeted specifically as somewhere that seems like a good place to work. In this chapter, we look at the steps you can take to get the job that is perfect for you.

I was talking recently to a woman who has the ideal job in a company she loves. She described the process she had gone through a number of years previously to get the position, and it sounded very rigorous indeed. She told me that while she was going through several rounds of interviews, it felt very tough, but once she joined the company she understood why they did things that way.

"It's a small team, in a business that is growing fast, and it is so important that we all get on, and work well together, apart from having the right skills and qualifications", she says. "The owners put a lot of time into choosing the right people, so that they settle well and really integrate."

The company, which is in learning and development, and is regionally based, has about 40 jobs currently on its website, and appears to have a great pipeline of work in hand. It is one of those small business success stories we all love to hear about.

And hats off to the owners who know that their success is all down to their people, and that the more time they invest in finding the right ones, the greater their success will be.

It is in great contrast to the 'hire easy, fire easy' approach of some concerns. If you pick up a job without breaking a sweat, the chances are you could be let go equally easily. So bear that in mind as you plan your strategy to land the perfect role.

Starting the Job Search

The obvious place to start looking is on jobs websites, right? Yes, I'm sure good roles have been found by starting there. But more often than not, people will report answering lots of advertisements and only getting a few acknowledgements. This is because advertisements on a jobs aggregator site are, of their nature, the widest possible trawl of the internet. They may get thousands of responses, so the only applicants who will get an answer are those who very, very specifically meet the exact requirements specified.

And this flies in the face of some of the received wisdom around job hunting which is to have a go, throw your hat in the ring, if you are not in, you can't win. We know that someone may just take a chance on you, even if you don't possess all the competencies specified, if you can reach them and impress them. I like to suggest to people I am coaching not to eliminate themselves before the prospective employer does.

You have to believe that even where you don't have all the experience specified, you might have transferrable skills that would adapt well.

Human Resources Director Audrey Cahill told me recently about the very strong internal recruiter she had in her last company. "She would always present 3 or 4 candidates who had been scored 90% by the algorithm, and who were very good in a subsequent preliminary interview, but she would also add to the short list one person who was a wild card", she says. "That person may have only scored 45% but very often they were the one who got the job. They had a curiosity or an enthusiasm that made us believe they would be a better long term fit."

So let's talk about reaching people, rather than just the search bots who are scanning the CVs on the jobs site.

Your Personal Network

A fantastic place to start is with friends, family, neighbours, distant cousins, the whole lot! Companies like the one mentioned above, the kind who value people – and probably the kind you want to work for let's face it - just love getting a recommendation from a member of staff. In fact, these personal recommendations are so valuable that many companies incentivise their staff with monetary bonuses when a friend or former class mate is hired.

So tell your former school and college mates, former colleagues, and friends of your family that you are job hunting, and ask them will they share your CV with their hiring teams. You will find those connections from your past quite easily on social media – most of us are fairly visible these days and easy to find. Personally I love when people from the past reach out to say hello, and if I can do any small thing for them or make an introduction I am glad to do so. Hopefully you too will get a positive response from your old contacts. Or at least an opportunity for a catch-up coffee or beer!

LinkedIn

Of all the social media platforms we engage in, LinkedIn is probably the most powerful in terms of job searching. Recruiters use it as a primary tool, and your presence there is key to how you will be found. Audrey Cahill mentions the Boolean search system that recruiters use on LinkedIn, and how internal recruiters use it to try to reach those candidates who have recently added the word 'jobseeker' before the commercial recruiters get to them!

She intends to recommend the creation of an internal recruitment team in her new role, one that will look beyond the algorithm where possible, to find people who really fit the culture - even where they mightn't tick all the boxes. She completed her own education later in life, and says she would never discount someone because they hadn't yet achieved qualifications, once they demonstrate a willingness to learn.

Career starters find LinkedIn strange at first, as they come to terms with a platform that is so different to the social channels they have used before. I have had lots of funny conversations with young people starting out on what 'likes' really mean, and how weird it is to be asking business people to 'friend' you.

You have to move past all of those ideas, and get into the networking frame of mind, where it is perfectly acceptable to ask people from every kind of business to connect with you, and where liking someone's post about work-life balance, or their sales drive, or the project they are working on is not so much personal, as respect for a good idea shared. It's not weird at all.

Your personal profile on LinkedIn should have:

- A good, clear, professional looking headshot

- A headline about who you are – the word Jobseeker will get you found easily

- A statement about your experience and qualifications

- A list of previous roles

- Education and qualifications

- Any memberships or volunteering.

Tip: Your LinkedIn profile is a work in progress, and it will change often, so remember to turn off the notifications to the network before you start. You don't want to notify the world and his granny every time you make a small change to your history.

Targeting A Specific Company or Concern

Where would you really, really like to work? What company or organisation stands out to you as somewhere that could be a good place to spend large chunks of your days?

Social media influencer and entrepreneur Shaan Puri posted something recently that really caught the wind. He said "Assume you get paid $1M per year no matter what you do, but you still gotta work 40 hours a week, what would you pick to work on?" It was astonishing how many of the thousands of answers he got were around teaching kids to do things differently, or creating communities. Purpose in what we do is increasingly important for most of us.

So identify a few concerns that interest you, and seem to have the kind of culture and purpose you want and check out their websites. Many organisations now have a recruitment section on their website with a notice saying that CVs will be accepted, even where they do not have specific jobs open at the moment.

Internal recruiters will tell you that they like receiving good cover emails and CVs from people who have identified their organisation as one they like, and who seem to have made it their business to find out as much about the business as they can. The internal recruiters or HR people never know when a current employee is going to hand in their notice, and leave a gap to be filled, so having a few applications already in the pipeline, or a few people they are already having exploratory conversations with is useful for them.

Once they get a sense that the candidate is aligned with their purpose.

Brian Murphy is Director of Employee Skilling at Microsoft, following previous high level positions in big pharma and banking.

"At Microsoft there are a number of things we hire against I was sent a video to view before my first day and that was about having a growth mindset, which told me all I needed to know about the orientation and the culture in the organisation" he says.

"In fact it was the only piece of content I was asked to look at, and therefore was presenting this as the most important thing. As a learning professional I was just so impressed with that positioning of this topic as we were preparing people for joining the company."

So if you are reaching out to that company you have identified as having the kind of culture and purpose you like, how should you do it?

Tough sales people used to be measured on their ability to make a cold call – a call to someone they had no previous contact with, using their best patter and persuasion to get a hearing. These days it is more likely to be a cold email, an email out of the blue, but which should be, in reality, far from cold.

Start by working out who is the correct person to write to. You might find HR managers, talent managers or hiring managers listed in the 'about us' section of the website. Search the company on LinkedIn and many of the people who work there, and their titles, will pop up.

Write a warm, friendly, but short email suggesting why you might be a good fit for their team. Refer to specific products or services they offer, places where you can contribute, so *they* know that *you* know who they are, and you are not mass emailing. Briefly touch on career achievements and qualifications, and then ask for a 15 minute chat, online or in person, so you can learn a little bit more about them.

Thank them for their time, attach your CV and think of a really good subject line, something that might encourage them to open the email in the first place. Before you hit send, proof read, and proof read again. First impressions count!

If you haven't heard anything back within a week or ten days, it is perfectly acceptable to send a follow up email. People are busy, they take holidays, and things get lost in the mass of information we receive every day.

Recruitment Companies

External recruiters work regularly with a stable of organisations, and build up strong relationships with the internal recruiting and HR teams. They submit applications in response to specific jobs contracted to them to fill, but they also submit - from time to time - details on a particular candidate who they think might fit the client company's culture or ethos. They might say 'This is someone you should keep an eye on, if you have anything coming up in the short term. I really think they would be a fit for you'.

So you need to research recruitment companies in your area - there are lots of them - to find the ones that seem to have a track record of placing people with your area of expertise. Then try to meet the recruiters in person, rather than just sending in a CV, or talking online, to see can you find one that you relate well to, and who might see your potential and put you forward for a few key interviews.

Mark Markey is co-founder with his wife Hazel of The Recruitment Bureau, a regional agency established twenty-seven years ago, now placing the children of the people they placed before, and indeed may have placed several times over their careers.

"It all comes down to relationships, both with the client and the candidate," he says. "Remember when jobs boards appeared first? They were going to be the agency killer. And then LinkedIn came, and it was going to be the agency killer. But we are still here".

The biggest change he has seen over the years is that, if you left a job without staying six or seven years in it, there was something wrong. Now there is something wrong if you stay more than three or four years! People move around very freely, and keep their CVs updated in readiness. And the agency will continue to be a key link between the client, the candidate and the hire.

"We are all part of the solution," Mark says. "Systems that will hunt through a CV – they are still fallible, they will still pick up someone's job from six or eight years ago and put them forward for something now on the basis of buzz words, and the candidate doesn't get anywhere.

"Whereas the agency, we can read between the lines, we can see the core competencies are there, but it is the other part – the soft skills, the tenacity, the resilience – that a skilled recruiter will see that the system can't. At the end of the day, it is a people-centred business, people making decisions about people".

The bottom line for a recruiter, Mark believes, is that a CV they send through to a client will definitely be read, even where it is speculative, whereas a candidate writing directly to a company, as we have described above, will have to be quite lucky or quite focused to get through.

Government Agencies

The most formal of all recruitment processes is probably those conducted by Government agencies. There are set steps to be gone through, with watertight cut off points, and very specific criteria to be met at each stage of the way. They don't allow for the more creative or 'have a go' approach we mentioned earlier, but do result in very secure, long-term roles which makes the process worth it for some.

These jobs are advertised by a central Government body, tasked with recruitment, and they will initially look for a registration of interest. I recently spoke to a young person who identified a role, and had the date to register noted in his diary. He logged on at 3.30pm and realised the system wouldn't accept it. They had closed the process at 3pm, not at a close of business that day, as he had thought they would, and that was that particular job gone for another year!

So the detail is paramount – the date and time to register interest is immovable. The initial registration is usually followed by an online questionnaire, again timebound, and if you get past that they look for your CV. Then you might then be called to a first interview, or further general knowledge or psychometric testing.

This can be followed by a second interview, and if successful you will be placed on a panel, and offered a job sometime in the subsequent months.

The Perfect CV

Search CV or Resumé templates online and you will find any number of clear styles you can use to organise your information. A lot of it is down to personal preference. So I'll leave you to do that in your own time, and will assume that you will choose a good layout and will proof read it well before your send it off. Here I want to focus on the content, what you say about yourself and how you say it.

Similar to the points we made about your LinkedIn profile earlier, whatever layout style you choose should include the following.

- Your name in bold on the top - not the word CV or Resumé, we know that is what is in front of us

- A clear descriptive headline, such as a client focused job seeker, or a recently qualified engineer, or an experienced coder

- A small, professional looking head shot

- A paragraph on who you are and what you are looking for

- Your experience, most recent job first and working back

- Your education , most recent first and working back

- Key skills

- Interests

The purpose of the CV is to set the agenda for the subsequent interview you will hopefully get invited to. How do we set the agenda? By presenting the information in a way that invites a positive question. And how do we do that? By referencing everything we have done as a positive achievement, rather than by presenting the information in a negative way, or by listing duties and responsibilities.

Far too many CVs received by organisations list the tasks the applicant completes every week in their current or previous role. Firstly, those things are what you are paid to do, so why list them off? And secondly, it gives far too many jump off points to an interviewer, reducing your control over the subsequent exchange. The following two examples of what I mean are from a senior and a more junior job seeker.

The senior applicant has a long and successful career at top management level. One previous role was when, a number of years ago, she ran her own consultancy firm. In the first CV we considered she had presented the headline as "The global economic crisis in 2009 necessitated a change of career, so I established the consultancy firm, ABC Inc."

And in the following detailed section she had "The services included Management, Finance, Accounting, Project Management, Procurement...." (and a lot more on a long list). This reads as a negative. Basically she is saying, "I had to set up a consultancy firm as I had nothing else on. I offered a whole range of services, in the hope that something would land."

The first question the interviewer will ask is, What happened? Were you fired from your last role? And then the long list gives the interviewer far too many options to choose from. What do you know about finance? What do you know about Project Management?

The interviewee will inevitably feel on the back foot throughout the process.

In the revised CV, we changed the headline to "Founded a strongly performing consultancy which achieved a powerful reputation and clients in the public and private sectors, including companies A, B, C and D".

We then listed achievements rather than services. "Became a key advisor to...; Designed and built a system for.....; Authored a report on....; Project managed a major acquisition for....."

Now imagine the questions the interviewer will ask. "So you set up your own firm, how was that for you?" And the interviewee gets the opportunity to talk about understanding business from that perspective, as a practitioner in the field, not just from the viewpoint of someone who has worked within a large concern or corporation all their working lives.

And the next question will be "Tell me about that acquisition you project managed, sounds very interesting". The way the information has been presented on the CV has changed the whole tone of the encounter.

The more junior job seeker had spent five years in the service industry, and was now looking to move to a more office based or career role. She had tried that once before, and it hadn't worked out, so she needed to present this information in a way that would read as a positive, not a negative.

Here's what we came up with. "Took a sabbatical from my long term role with Delvin Retail when selected for a three month internship with (big company) designed to allow young people from different backgrounds try out financial services". And we listed her achievements as report writing, developing great office skills, learning about company investigation and so on.

She can now present this information in the context of someone curious, who landed a good opportunity and tried it out, but found it was not for her. So she took the learning back to her old role where her new understanding of business and finance supported the back end of the retail operation. She continued as a valued member of the team, but is now moving to a new location where she would like to use her experience, and her proven ability to work in a pressurised environment, to find a customer service role in an office setting.

It is so important to be truthful on the CV, not to claim things you haven't done, but it is perfectly acceptable to present your information in the best light, in order to set yourself up for a positive interview experience. And remember, *do not* say you love reading if you can't discuss the last book you read.

Tip: Do not list current or past duties and responsibilities in a CV, you were paid to do those things. Present your information as achievements and learnings.

Preparing for Interview

No matter what role you are going for, or how strong your education and experience, you must realise there are many other candidates out there who are just as well qualified as you. So how do you set yourself apart from them? You find things that are unique to you, and make sure to bring them into the interview, in a way that makes you memorable.

One time when I was sitting on a job interview panel for a large organisation, over the course of a day we met about ten recent graduates with similar backgrounds and experience. I thought the HR team had done a great job and had found really good candidates. They were all fantastic in different ways, and I would have loved to have given all of them a job.

But one candidate stood out. When asked about his experience of taking initiative, or running a project, he spoke about a summer job he had held in a bar in a regional town, where custom had been declining for a good while. He had asked the manager could he run an X Factor night for local charities one night a week for ten weeks, and had persuaded all the local clubs, choirs and bands to put acts forward.

The idea took off, with the whole community getting behind it, and the pub began to take in more on that night of the week then the whole of the rest of the week put together.

The candidate told the story in a fairly modest way, but you knew it genuinely had been his own idea, that he had put huge effort into it, and that it had worked really well. When we came to the end of the day, our candidate discussion lasted about ten seconds. We each said "X Factor guy" without hesitation and he got the job.

In order to get ready for an interview, you need to think about what you are going to say and how you are going to say it.

The interview chart below will help. An hour spent on this chart will completely change the way you perform at the interview.

WHAT	HOW	THE NASTY	QUESTIONS
Key messages 1 2 3 4	Examples and stories 1 2 3 4	The question you don't want to be asked. Prepare a good answer and bring it up before they do.	1 2 3 4 5 6 7 ... As many more questions as you can think of!

Step 1

Of all the things you have done so far in your career, what are you most proud of? Note your top three or four in the What column. These are your key messages, the things you are going to talk about in the interview, come hell or high water. In other words, you are not going to leave the room until you get these things said, as they are the things that show you in best light.

Step 2

For each key message you want to get across, match it with a couple of examples or stories that prove you did what you claim to have done. Our friend above didn't claim to have improved the turnover of the pub, he told a great story that showed he had done exactly that. The story was strong, authentic and completely memorable.

Step 3

Think about the nasty question, the one question you would hate the interviewer to ask you. Maybe it is the gap in your career, maybe it is the business that failed, maybe it is the time you dropped out of college? Write it down, and think of how you are going to bring it up before the interviewer does. Because by doing that, you get to discuss it on your terms, not in a defensive way.

Step 4

List off as many questions as you can think of that the interviewer might ask you. Now pick a question, any question, and practice giving a good answer to that question, but also seamlessly moving on to talk about one of your key messages. This is easier than it sounds. In normal conversation, we move from topic to topic linking them quite naturally. Finish the answer to the question by giving an example, or telling a brief story that shows what you are saying is true. Continue on through the questions you have prepared, randomly picking them from the list, answering them well, but always continuing on to one of your strong points.

Tip: Practice your answers out loud! Yes, you will get some strange looks from your house mates, but it is worth it. Hearing yourself give good answers in your practice session will allow you to be much more confident in the interview.

Practicing your Answers

I often get asked, what is the right length for an answer to a question at interview. How do you know you are not being too short in your replies, or worse, being far too long and waffly? If you use the pattern above for each answer, it will sound right to your own ears, and you will feel the correct length to the answer. It is a bit like knowing the music as well as the words to a song.

So take the example of the early career person mentioned above, transitioning from the retail industry to the office environment. She might be asked, "How confident are you with using Excel? There can't have been much use for it in your retail job?"

She says the following:

> "Well I didn't use it every day, but I am quite good at it from when I did that internship in the big company, and I'm sure it will come back to me if I have to use it more often".

The answer is a bit short, it is not going anywhere, and it allows the interviewer straight back in with another rapid fire question, which risks making the whole pace of the interview too fast, and even a bit defensive.

Or she could try this:

> "When I learned to use it every day during the three months I spent with the big company, I found it very easy to navigate and because I had also used some of the more complex features

I brought it back to the ordering system in the shop. One day we had this huge order come in, with all kinds of different products, and I inputted everything as it was being unloaded. So we knew exactly what was there, and I was able to track things as they ran out and re-order them without any delay. The owners were delighted with the efficiency, which they had never had before, and I was happy to be keeping up to date with my skills".

Boom!

In this answer you are saying you are inventive, innovative, happy to suggest new ways of doing things, and offering so much more than an interviewer can later pick up on.

Answering interview questions is a bit like playing chess. You have to be thinking a few moves ahead, feeding into this answer something that you want the interviewer to be curious about, and come to in their next question, so you can bring it into your next answer.

The Preliminary Interview

With so much emphasis these days on company culture, and finding people who are the right fit, there may well be several rounds to the interview process. It is great to be called to the first interview, often conducted online and often conducted by a recruitment agent or internal recruiter.

Don't underestimate the seriousness of this step. People who are interviewing every single day in this way are very skilled, and very adept at reading people. They are looking firstly for veracity – it is likely that what you have put on the CV is a fair representation of what you have actually done in the past?

Then they are looking for attitude, energy, enthusiasm and knowledge about the job or company being applied for. They will not put you forward to the next round, no matter how well qualified you are, without feeling confident that you have done your homework and that you know something about the organisation and what will be expected of you there.

If they are recommending you to go forward, they have to stand over you as one of their choices, and they don't want to be let down. A friendly, enthusiastic, curious approach goes a long way. Don't be afraid to ask lots of questions, as well as answering the ones you are asked.

Remember that an interview is just a conversation with a purpose. It is two equals meeting to explore are you a fit for this organisation; and is this organisation a fit for you, and will it give you the career and personal development you are looking for?

The Competency Based Interview

This interview follows a set pattern and has been designed to elicit very specific information about each candidate, but also to be completely fair and transparent as to why someone is chosen to go through to the next round. Bigger organisations have been known to favour this approach, as a number of interviewers can work separately through the pile of applicants, knowing that everyone will be asked the same questions, and scored in the same way.

The interviewer is advised to be sure to welcome the candidate to the interview, and to create a nice atmosphere to allow the candidate to relax and settle into the process. They are told how much time to allocate to each section of the interview, and they are given specific positives and negatives to look out for in relation to each capability. Afterwards, they fill in a specific matrix, drawn up by the HR or recruiting teams.

In the example below, the interviewers were directed to:

1. Ask a couple of warm up questions. Tell us a bit about yourself? What attracts you to this role? What do you know about this role? - 5 minutes

2. Select 2 of the prescribed questions for each of the five capabilities to ask the candidate - 30 minutes

3. Ask a one or two closing questions. Why do you want this role? What would your current manager say is your strongest point? Do you have any questions for us? – 5 minutes

Capability Based Interview Scoring Matrix

Candidate Name:	Date:
Assessor Name:	

	Capability	Score (1-5)
	Customer Focus	
	Accountability	
	Collaboration	
	Demonstrates Self Awareness	
	Vision and Purpose	

	1	2	3	4	5
OVERALL PERFORMANCE	☐ VERY WEAK	☐ NEEDS DEVELOPMENT	☐ SATISFACTORY	☐ STRONG	☐ VERY STRONG
RECOMMENDED HIRE	☐ YES	☐ NO			

Key Strengths and Development recommendations
A summary of the candidate's key strengths and development areas based on their performance in the interview.

SCORE

After completing the interviews, the interviewer submits all the reports to the central recruiting team, who feel that regardless of how many separate interviewers may have been in the pool, all the candidates will have been given the same questions, and the same amount of time to respond to them.

It is not a very flexible approach, but can indeed be deemed to be fair. The onus is on the interviewee to be as creative as possible within the framework that has been set, and to use the example based approach to answering a question outlined earlier as well as you can.

Interestingly, the more senior the role, the more complex the format will be, and the more onus there will be on the interviewers to be absolutely transparent and above board.

When I sat on an interview board for a very senior role in broadcasting, I was interested to see the Chair ask at the end of the few days for all of our handwritten notes and jottings, along with the formal reports we had filled in. Our scribblings were to be sealed into the envelope, along with the formal report for each candidate, to be locked away in a secure safe in case of a legal challenge any time in the future!

The Panel Interview

When an interview panel is convened, usually for a more senior role, a Chair is appointed and he or she will decide on the approach they are going to take. They will sometimes divide up the topics, deciding that one person will ask about finance, the second person about marketing, the third person about leadership, and so on. Usually the Chair does the opening questions, and also does the closing questions.

But on occasion a more fluid approach has been

decided, and questions land on the candidate from all sides and in any order. So you have to be ready for whatever approach they take and roll with the punches.

By the time it gets to a panel, you are probably on a short list, and your experience of the first couple of rounds will have told you plenty about the organisation and their culture. You will also have a really clear idea of whether this is the right role for you, and your growing enthusiasm should give you a good edge to deliver your best performance on the day.

Candidates who are successful at this final stage will often tell you that the knowledge that they were down to the wire made them more free in what they said. They didn't worry about seconding guessing what the panel might want to hear, and concentrated instead on saying things that were honest, insightful and memorable.

One senior candidate said to me, "I knew at that stage that if they didn't like my ideas for the department, I wouldn't want to work for them. I could see clearly what had to be done to turn things around, and if they weren't going to back me on that, I wouldn't be happy there". She got the job, and by all accounts has made a real difference.

Your best pointers for planning for a panel interview are:

1.   Find out who is on the panel. Knowing a little about each person can give you perspective as you frame your answers.

2.   Have your content developed further, they will want to delve deeper now

3.   Walk into the room confidently

4.   Repeat each name as you are introduced, "Good to meet you John; Thanks for having me here today Linda; I'm looking forward to our chat Jennifer."

5.   Settle into your seat, and look open and interested

6.   Give your first answer, remembering to spread your eye contact around the table

7.   As the questions move on, refer back to earlier points. "Yes, I believe the strategy is really important, John, and it speaks to the question Jennifer asked earlier about people management…" This shows you are really listening, and are in confidently in command of the whole communication.

8.   Clarify what is being looked for if need be before answering. "Is your concern Linda around the timing of the project or the budget? I'm happy to address either".

9.   Watch out for two part questions, and start your answer in a way that reminds yourself where you are going. "I'll address the financial reporting first and then go on to the compliance issues."

10. Ask questions of them. It is a lot more expected and accepted than it used to be

11. Share your vision for the role, the department or the business

Have a really strong ending prepared. When they start to wrap up, thank them for having you and say something like ,"I want to leave you with a thought, if I may. I believe the future success of this team/department/ business will depend on......I have given this so much thought over the last few weeks as we have been going through this process, and I believe I am the right person for you, and will make a big difference if you give me the opportunity."

The final point is one of the most important ones. You have to let them know you really, really want this job and are prepared to ask for it. You wouldn't believe how many people do interviews without remembering to ask for the job!

⌘

They say it is a job seekers market at the moment, with many, many roles open in the developed world. However, that can change at any time as inflation kicks in, energy prices fluctuate, and the tech world takes another wobble. Regardless of the state of the world economy, finding the right role takes effort and commitment and a systematic approach to researching opportunities and going after them.

It also takes a fairly clean social media profile.

It is estimated that 70% of employers check a candidate's online presence before calling them to interview or offering them a job. Of course it shouldn't matter what you do in your spare time, but the fact is it probably does. So go back over your timeline and get rid of the student hi-jinks photos, and the now not-so-funny tags your dear friends have nailed you with. Check your comments and shares, up your privacy levels and generally tidy things up. You may be very glad you did.

Chapter Four

Presenting and Public Speaking

In this chapter you will find everything you need to prepare and deliver a great talk. You'll understand the speaker/audience dynamic, the things that go wrong, and then you'll have a blueprint to follow to make sure your own next outing is nothing short of stellar!

He is a tech multi-millionaire who travels the world keeping up with all his investments, and who gets asked to deliver keynote speeches quite regularly.

He came bounding into our office one day looking for help with a presentation he was making in China the following week. He was due to have a 20 minute slot, in front of an international audience.

"I have 68 slides in my deck," he told me cheerfully.

Oh, help us all, I thought, it is going to be a long morning.

So over the course of that session and another one a couple of days later, we completely re-worked his presentation. He ended up with something good, aimed specifically at his audience, and with some very clear easy messages for them to take away.

Oh yes, and I allowed him to keep eight slides! It was plenty.

Ever since we first sat around a campfire and began telling stories, we have honoured and respected those who can capture the human condition and share it with the rest of us.

We fall silent and listen to those who can move or inspire or inform or delight us with their choice of words and their command of language. We can become absolutely mesmerised when the orator also understands and uses body language, facial expressions, gestures, stage-craft, audience skills, pauses, vocal inflections, humour, drama – and a whole raft of other effective tools there for the taking.

The problem is that a lot of people don't bother with these tools, and rely instead on hiding behind the dreaded slides, as we discussed in the last chapter, sending us all to sleep before the third bullet point is on the screen.

My other personal pet hate is the presenter who starts his talk by telling us what he is going to tell us, how he is going to tell it, and what reaction he expects us to have. This is a dreary kind of housekeeping that announces loudly to us that right now is a very good time to do some texting or check emails.

It was a format for starting a talk that was suggested by Dale Carnegie back in the 1950s and it is quite extraordinary that some presentation trainers are still telling people that it works today. Believe me, it doesn't.

Remember Renée Zellweger's great line from the movie Jerry Maguire where she played opposite Tom Cruise: "You had me at hello"?

That's how you need to start a talk or presentation in the give-it-to-me-up-front world of today. You need to grab our attention from the get go, make us believe in you, and then take us on a compelling journey.

Presenting and speaking is a learned craft. No one did it brilliantly the very first time they stood up there and tried. But absolutely everyone can raise their bar and improve substantially. It takes a few techniques, some practice and a good understanding of how to control nerves, as described already.

A 'feel the fear and do it anyway' kind of attitude helps too.

I was coaching a woman one time who was the second-in-command in the marketing department of a multinational. She decided that for her own career progression she ought to step up and make the main presentation at the annual conference, a role that her team lead had undertaken in the past few years.

So she went up to the CEO to put the case, a little nervously, that her colleague had done the job very well last year, and the year before, and that it might be time to have a fresh presenter with fresh views?

Without batting an eyelid the CEO said yes, absolutely, great idea, the job is yours this year, and don't worry, I'll square it with the team lead.

My friend left the office, and actually had to lean up against the wall outside because of the wave of panic that almost knocked her over. She had not expected to get a yes to her proposal so easily, and having never spoken in public before, now had to deliver in front of a tough audience of her peers.

So we worked hard on the presentation, and got her a practice run in front of a small but very supportive business network. And then she did the presentation at the conference, in front of 300 people, to a great reaction.

She was absolutely thrilled that her decision to push herself, and to put in the work, achieved her goal of raising her personal profile within her organisation.

The Key to a Good Speech

All good presentations and speeches begin with one essential piece of understanding, and that is the fact that we absorb, understand and remember spoken communication very differently to how we absorb written communication.

So think about this for a moment. If you carefully research and write up a paper, intended for publication, and read it out verbatim at a conference, don't be surprised to look up from your reading to find your audience nodding off to sleep, checking mobiles or even getting up and leaving half way through.

You are asking them to do something they are not physically equipped to do – to absorb aurally material that you carefully designed to be absorbed visually and analytically.

The exceptions in your audience are those who have pre-read your paper and have made notes, so they can ask intelligent questions or indeed challenge the content of your paper. They might be relied on to give you a bit of eye contact. As may the few who have the paper printed out in front of them and are reading along with you.

So if this is the case, how then do audio books work? Or how do the visually impaired learn from the written word?

Well, authors of popular novels, the kind that are often found in audio book form, are usually great story-tellers. Their narrative style and choice of words is deliberately lyrical, descriptive and colourful, giving us a very full sensory experience. We do not only understand the words, we are prompted to paint pictures in our own heads, bringing the characters, places and scenarios to life.

Add to that a good recording from a skilled actor as narrator, and you layer on the potential for plenty more interpretation and meaning.

And compare that now with my hapless academic and his paper, wondering why the tops of people's heads are the only thing he can see in the auditorium.

He is working with material that is probably very worthy, but on the dry side, and he does not have the descriptive skill of the novelist, or the delivery skills of an actor. So he doesn't stand a chance.

To turn a paper into a decent talk he needs to do the brave thing and leave the script back home on the desk. He needs to work from personal memory and create for the audience an aural experience that will pull them in with pictures and emotion and connection, so they will look up and start listening.

The same goes for the corporate presenter who thinks it is all about the slide deck. She is also asking her audience the impossible.

She is asking them to squint up at facts and figures, graphs and slides and to take in material in a way that they are not physically equipped to do. This is material she could easily share with them online, or give out later on a cheat sheet. And all the while she is missing the opportunity of the presentation to win hearts and minds and get some real reaction.

We have all heard poor speakers, and have completely zoned out while they are on the platform, wishing we had not sat so close to the front where it was impossible to slip out unnoticed! Actually, we are quite selfish as listeners. We want to know straight away what is in this for me?

The things that make us zone out are usually:

Irrelevancy – Talk is not addressing my needs

Boredom – I can't stay focused

Complexity – I can't follow what he is on about

Density – Too much material

No examples – I don't get it

Monotone delivery – She's sending me to sleep

Connection missing – He's not reaching out to me

Credibility lack – She has not made it clear why I should listen

Discomfort – I don't like his obvious unease

Personality missing – I can't get a sense of who she is

Good speakers, on the other hand, speak to you as if you are the only person in the room. They use conversational language, which is easy to listen to and easy to understand. They capture your attention immediately, and hold it throughout the talk. They look and sound relaxed and in control.

The talk is colourful, interesting and informative. When it comes to the end, you realise it had a structure and a purpose to it, and you experience a feeling of satisfaction.

In very simple terms, most good talks follow the same pattern. They have a big opening, a number of clear messages, which are illustrated well, and a big closing. The closing may in some way circle back to the opening, which adds to that notion of satisfaction.

If you were to draw a diagram for a good talk, it would look like this:

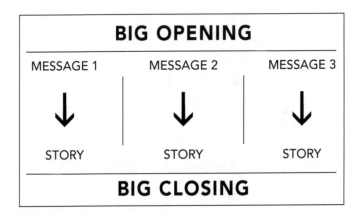

The Big Opening

is where you jump straight in with a story, an unusual or intriguing fact, some drama, a question, a demand – anything but housekeeping.

The idea is to catch the attention immediately and make them think, this is going to be good, I'm really glad I came in to this session.

Comedians often start with the line, "A funny thing happened on the way in to the theatre tonight." Of course we know it didn't happen that day, but we enjoy the immediacy and the sense of a story about to begin so we pay attention.

Then the talk goes on to its key messages, each one illustrated with an anecdote or a story.

And it finishes up with a Big Closing, often something visionary or uplifting, which gets the audience thinking about the future, and how things will be from now on.

We often describe the prepared closing in a talk as a Parachute. It is the place you go to when the chairperson of the event tinkles the glass to tell you to wrap up, and you take a minute or two to finish up strongly. You have your parachute ready, it opens up, and allows you to land well. You don't panic, when you come to the end of your time, and stop dead.

There is nothing worse at the end of a talk than a lame fade out, the speaker saying, "So, em, I think... em... that's where I'll finish up... em... maybe... em..." Pause.

And then a hopeful, "I wonder are there any questions?"

Or the other scenario where the speaker has three or four endings, one after the other, and the audience begins to get very restless and uncomfortable.

I once attended a conference, where one of the speakers was clearly reading out a script, I saw the Chair signal to her that her time was up. She nodded, but kept on reading.

She read another full page, and turned another page, and another one, and another one, completely ignoring the now frantic signals from the Chair. The audience was at this stage coughing, shifting in the seats, sighing, checking mobile phones and showing all the usual signs that they are losing the will to live.

The speaker clearly had no interest in the comfort of her audience, and no ability to summarise what she was about, or to go to a good strong closing when her agreed time was up. It is unprofessional, and it is also inconsiderate to the event organisers and the other speakers.

Good speakers are deeply concerned about their audience. In fact they know that the audience always comes first, regardless of the type of talk or presentation to be made.

Preparing the Talk

So here it is, the ten-step, three-phase approach to the perfect presentation, the one that will allow you to shine as a really good communicator.

The Thinking Phase: Audience, Message and Goal

1. Audience

Where do you do your best thinking? In the bath? On the treadmill? Walking the dog? Driving home in the evening? Wherever it is, that is the place where your talk begins to emerge, your ideas start to take shape, and your objectives begin to become clear.

A good talk starts with the audience, not with the list of things you want to say. In the corporate world, people often have difficulty with this one.

I hear people saying all the time, "Oh but I have to present the results", or "I have to outline the plans for the coming year", or "I have to tell them all about the sales drive." Of course you do, but you have to tell it in a way that is relevant and interesting to them, or you may as well save yourself the bother, because they will just drift off while you are speaking.

You start by really thinking about your audience, and asking yourself who exactly are they, why will they be there on the day and what will their expectations be? Although you will be the person on the platform, in the spotlight, they are actually the important people in the room, not you. You are just the conduit for the message.

So you research your audience and what they might already know about the topic, or what they still need to find out. You also need to get a handle on what they know about you as the speaker or presenter of the subject, and what they perceive your expertise to be.

You need to establish whether the audience is more less coming from the one place, or whether it comprises different interest groups and stakeholders, in which case your message will have to impact on a few different levels.

Tip: What is the hook that will grab this audience, unite them and engage them to really listen to the message.

2. Message

Now think about the message or messages you want to get across. This is often quite clear in the case of company targets and objectives, but a bit more obscure when you are dreaming up a topic for that TED talk. Or when you are trying to think of a way of engaging an audience with your social enterprise so they will become involved, or contribute in some way.

Your messages should be distinct and clear, and when planning them, you should keep reminding yourself that less is more. Better that your audience take one clear thought on board that they fully understand and act upon, rather than hearing loads of facts that have no impact at all.

Tip: With messaging, less is more

3. Goal

You then have to ask yourself, what do you want this audience to do as a result of listening to you, and hearing these messages. That is your goal.

Do you want them to be motivated, or inspired, or entertained? To hire you or to buy your product? To be enlightened or informed? To become an advocate for a cause or spread a message?

So by the end of your thinking phase, you should have worked out how your messages at point 2 will be designed so that the audience at point 1 will allow you to achieve your goal at point 3.

Tip: Be clear on the goal of your presentation

And now you know what you want to achieve, so you are ready to start mapping out your presentation.

The Preparing Phase – Mapping, Blocking, Linking, Re-sequencing

4. Mapping

So how do you start putting your thoughts on paper?

You can use a mind map, dumping all your thoughts and ideas on a big sheet, with boxes and charts and clouds and arrows going everywhere. You can scribble a few thoughts on the back of a beer mat. You can open the laptop and type furiously, getting it all out of your head and onto the screen. You can knock yourself out with bullet points. You can write it out in longhand.

It doesn't actually matter at all which method you choose, once you assemble the information somewhere, to see what you have got. Research comes into play here, allowing you to support your information with facts.

Tip: Capture your thoughts in the way that works for
you

5. Blocking

Now you have to get the thoughts corralled into themes and logical blocks of information, starting work on the examples and illustrations you will use to make each block come alive.

This is really important. You have to have a very clear idea of how you are going to get each idea across.

That means the actual anecdote or description you'll use will not only make your material really interesting for the audience, but it will also help you remember it.

Tip: Decide on your blocks, and match each one with a good example of what you are talking about, something you have experienced personally.

6. Linking

In delivering a speech, people rarely get lost in the blocks, particularly if they have a good story attached. But they can get confused in the links. Good talks flow smoothly from one idea to the next, the links connecting the blocks in a natural way.

Think about your links, the couple of sentences that will connect the last idea to the next one smoothly. This is what a continuity announcer does on television, or a DJ does on the radio. They take us seamlessly from one programme or song to the next one, somehow connecting them in our minds.

Links are all about Content, Context and Continuity.

Tip: You will know you have your links right when they make your talk flow smoothly.

7. Re-sequencing

You may find that certain blocks, no matter how you link them, don't flow into one another. So change the blocks around. Play with them until you are happy that you have found ways of getting them to connect up in several different ways.

This is where a lot of people get their talk preparation wrong. When we write, we usually follow a logical sequence, and assume that we have to deliver the talk in this sequence. But actually we don't. No one in the audience knows how you originally mapped things out, and it may work better in a different way.

David Bowie says the lyrics from some of his best songs resulted from experimenting with chopped up sentences and rearranged lines. In the same way, you may need to move the furniture about, to give your room a different look!

Tip: You can give yourself great comfort in knowing that your blocks work equally well in several different ways.

The Practising Phase – Headings, Vocalising, Visualising

8. Headings

After you have reconstructed your talk, and are really happy that your blocks are a moveable feast, think of headings that will identify each block. The heading should be a meaningful idea. It should refer to the illustration of the message, and not to an abstract point.

It is possible to give a great twenty minute talk with no notes at all other than a few headings on a prompt card or on your iPad but the headings have to be meaningful. If your heading is 'marketing' or 'financials', there is a danger that in the heat of the moment you might not remember what you were going to say.

Much better to have a heading that prompts you to tell the story about Mike's great marketing drive last year, or a heading that suggests you describe how the big sale was won, or even the punchline to a good story.

Tip: Choose meaningful headings for your prompts.

9. Vocalising

Saying chunks of the talk out loud is very important. Driving home in the evening, or on that treadmill again, you need to hear yourself trying out the stories you will tell, so you can refine them, and avoid rambling.

But it is equally important not to give the whole talk too often from start to finish, or you will start learning off pieces, and begin to put yourself into the learned memory zone, rather than keeping the talk in personal memory.

Over-rehearsing, or learning things off by heart, causes a speaker to come across as scripted and false. The best speakers work really hard to sound natural and spontaneous.

Tip: When vocalising your blocks to hear how they sound, do them singly and not in order.

10. Visualising

I think it is obvious at this stage that you should promise yourself that you will never, ever again start a presentation by opening up your laptop and going to slide one! Starting there is shooting yourself in the foot, locking yourself into a linear presentation that prevents you from giving of your best.

But if, at this point in your talk preparation, it is clear that some concepts need something else to connect with the audience, then you think about a visual – a picture or illustration - that will bring the point home, or make the audience smile, or even wonder what this is about.

Death by PowerPoint is one of the curses of modern business life. Slides should only ever be used when they serve a genuine purpose – to enhance the communication. Unfortunately they are used every day all over the world for no reason at all except that people mistakenly think they will look unprepared if they show up without them.

Tip: Ask yourself is the slide there for you, as a personal prompt, or is it there for the audience?

Preparing yourself

Doing the work, as described above, puts you in a great place to tackle a talk. You are setting yourself up for success by using a system that frees you up to showcase the best version of yourself, not a machine who looks and sounds like he swallowed the corporate manual before he went up on stage.

The best version of yourself is the person you really are – the person your friends and family see every day. There is no better version of you. That's it. That's the one.

It's fully honest, and if you are honest you will know that the smiles, applause and any other affirmation you get is fully deserved. It is for the real you.

I describe it as 'wearing the bus driver's hat' when someone presents in a way they think is expected of them, rather than in a way that is true to themselves. They think that when representing the company or the organisation they need to look and sound and act like the bus driver. So they plant the hat firmly on their heads and tie up their communication in language they never normally use.

The alternative is to be yourself, to focus so strongly on meeting the needs of the audience and on delivering understandable messages, that your true self shines out, and your enthusiasm and passion for the subject lights up the room.

This is authentic presentation, the best kind of public speaking possible.

I need to know you if I am going to listen to you, and if I am going to do what you ask of me. And the only way I can get to know you, as a speaker, is if I can see you. So you have to have the confidence to let me see you.

You let me see you by sharing some detail about yourself as you speak but, and this is a really big but, that is not to be confused with talking about yourself.

You use yourself to make a point, to share an insight, to show that it is just the same for you, but not to brag, or big yourself up, or try to impress.

I have listened to many talks from people on the business speaking circuit who have misunderstood this. They are asked to speak at Chamber of Commerce or Women in Business events to share their story, and they think that this is an open invitation to talk about themselves for an hour.

"I went to college in ... and then I went to America for a few years... And then I came home and set up my business ... And I have been hugely successful. ... And I think it is easy to do and anyone can do it..." Blah, blah, blah!

As a listener, the only thing going through your mind as they ramble on is, "And your point is?"

What is happening is that the speaker is getting bogged down with information, while the audience is looking for insight.

An experienced speaker understands that when you are invited to come to an event to share your story, you are really being asked to use yourself as a means to show what you have learned along the way. What are the things you would do differently if you had your time again, for example.

You give vignettes from your own story to show experience and empathy, and to build a bridge across which the audience can travel, but that is definitely not to be confused with self-indulgence!

And the best speakers are always looking to improve, to raise their personal bar. They never sit back and convince themselves that they have this thing cracked, and they don't need to work on it any more. After every single outing, they choose someone they respect to give them honest feedback.

The Panel Discussion

Have you noticed that panel discussions have become really popular at conferences? Event planners and conference organisers are clearly reacting to bad speakers and Death by PowerPoint and are working hard to make these occasions more enjoyable for all of us.

So after the opening address and the first keynote from the podium, you will usually find an armchair setting with an MC or Moderator to introduce a panel of speakers and to field some questions.

For those planning seminars and kick-offs, it is a great way of changing the pace and tone, breaking up the main presentations and getting more people onto the platform. This varies the voices and the points of view, and of course gets good questions and interactivity from the audience.

For speakers, it is a great opportunity to take part in an event in a less pressurised way than delivering a thirty or forty-minute speech. The only disadvantage to it is that you have a much shorter time to get your message out.

And there may also be someone who is an industry expert but an inexperienced Chair in the moderator role, and they can allow one speaker to dominate, or fail to keep the topics moving along.

When you agree to take part in a panel, you take your chances!

Depending on the format, each panellist can be asked to make a short stand-alone presentation, followed by the question and answer session. Or sometimes the whole panel discussion is simply a series of questions and answers, with no overview piece beforehand.

So if the panel segment is running from 10am to 11 am, and each panellist has been asked to speak for about 6 minutes first, the Moderator's running order will look something like this:

10.00	Introduction of topic and speakers.
	Call first speaker
10.03	Speaker 1
10.10	Introduce Speaker 2
10.12	Speaker 2
10.20	Introduce Speaker 3
10.22	Speaker 3
10.30	Introduce Speaker 4
10.32	Speaker 4
10.40	Begin Q & A
10.58	Wrap Up

You can see how tight it is, and how the Moderator will have to work really hard to get everyone started and finished promptly, so that there will be time left for the Q & A, and the all-important audience involvement.

In a six-minute talk, allowing a minute or two of grace as we have set out above, you will really only get across one or maybe two messages. Better to say one or two things that will resonate and be remembered, rather than running through a list of things that will be forgotten immediately you leave the stage.

So you should use the same format described earlier as regards the big opening and the big closing, but confine yourself to a lot less material in the middle.

The clock is everything in a panel discussion. Take your mobile with you, on silent, place it on the podium beside you, use the stop watch, and finish up within a minute of your time – simple professionalism and courtesy.

The presentation part out of the way, you then have to think about the Q & A, and how you can use the opportunity to reinforce some messaging from your talk, or to make some new points that were not covered.

I was working with the leadership team in a major tech firm who had decided that the previous year's annual conference had been a bit dull so they wanted to do something different this year.

They told me that previously they each had to present to the audience of 1,000 people a short piece on their area of responsibility, something they were very familiar with, and which should not have been a problem. However, the event team had micromanaged the whole day, and the speakers had felt over-scripted, locked in to set-piece contributions, and very awkward to the point of having their credibility undermined in front of the business.

They were determined not to let the same thing happen again.

So we decided that this year the session with the team leaders should be a panel discussion, with a TV personality as MC. We worked on simplifying their messages down to a vision for what each department could achieve, an expression of belief in the team to deliver the vision, and a couple of specific asks from the leader so that the vision could start rolling out.

That gave a structure and an intent to every response the leader would make, regardless of where the TV presenter might find inspiration for his question, or where he might decide to take the conversation.

Then we began working on key messages which each leader would build in to his or her replies, and a story or illustration to match each message to show how this would benefit the team and make their work easier.

The last thing was agreeing that no one would use notes, so that the leaders would really listen to the questions and the whole conversation, so they could support each other if necessary and keep the session sounding very casual and informal, despite the strong messages that were to be delivered.

Afterwards, I heard that it had gone very well. The team said they had really enjoyed the occasion, done the job well and, more importantly, that they had come across as themselves.

A panel discussion, like the one described here, is a bit like doing a media interview. The questions can come from anywhere, and you have to be prepared to tackle the issue in hand, while moving it on to one of your key messages.

A good way to think about it is to remember that each of your answers is supposed to aid the understanding of the audience. So use the word **AID** to remind you to:

Address

Illustrate

Direct

Address the issue you have been asked about. That is slightly different to trying to answer the question, which you may not be able to do, if you don't have the facts to hand.

You can always offer to find the facts and send them on later, but in the meantime you have a great opportunity to address the issue, bringing insight that otherwise might not have been thought about by anyone there, and to skilfully start bringing your contribution around to one of your messages.

Illustrate what you mean. Share an anecdote or find a good analogy to introduce colour and description to what are you saying, which immediately makes the message completely understandable to the audience and anchors it in their minds. If your anecdote is good enough, this is what they will be talking about at the coffee break, your message having gone home, straight and true.

Direct the end of your answer to another one of your messages, using key words to place a hook in the mix for the Moderator to pick up on. By that I mean as you finish off your answer, say something like, "That's why people always wonder where we source the products, and how we get them here on time".

It absolutely begs the question, well where do you source the products, and how do the logistics work?

Using the AID system of answering does a few things.

It takes the fear out of any question that might be thrown at you. You will not be stuck, you have a system to use and will always be able to give a credible answer.

It also allows you to really focus on what is going on, in the moment, and to be fully mindful of what your fellow panellists are saying, rather than shutting them out so you can rehearse your own answer! You look stronger as a panellist when you are able to refer to something your colleague has just said, and build on it within your own answer.

So a panel discussion is not a solo run. It is a joint contribution. To my mind you should act like you remember that while you are on the platform, or you might not get asked back.

≫

Most of us will never reach the public speaking heights of a JFK, or a Martin Luther King who undoubtedly had the benefit of brilliant speech writers, but who were themselves the very definition of excellent communicators.

They not only put the audience first, planned great messages, gave brilliant examples, showed their vulnerability, and were fully authentic – but they understood rhythm and timing. And they were able to perform and deliver to a very high level the constructs the speech writers worked in.

Typical constructs are phrases of three – left, right and centre; the good the bad and the ugly; on the beaches, on the streets and in the air – or phrases of opposites – to be or not to be; on the one hand or on the other; when the going gets tough, the tough get going.

That last one originated from Pierre Salinger, speech writer for Bobby Kennedy, not singer Billy Ocean, as many people seem to think!

Working musicality and cadence of this level into your speech is premiership stuff, and perhaps beyond the reach of a lot of us, but it is a fascinating subject, and well worth reading up on.

Why not try out one in your next speech and see how it sounds?

Chapter Five

Becoming Pitch Perfect

Pitching has become something of an art form. It is that activity we have to undertake if we want to win business, make a sale, attract finance, or win support for a project. In this chapter we explore how it is done.

The 'Paper' Pitch

A pitch often starts with an email to an investor or manager hoping for support for a project, product or service. Unfortunately on too many occasions the pitch is written so badly it ends in the virtual trash can.

I don't think it is an exaggeration to say that 90 per cent of them start like this:

> 'My name is John and I do such and such... I attended college in... degree in biochemistry... In my career I have done all kinds of interesting things... I am passionately interested in entrepreneurship... My product is going to change the world... I plan to take it here, there and everywhere... Can we meet for a coffee so I can tell you how you can help me?'

Or from the charity or social enterprise is like this:

> 'We are the society for the betterment of humankind... We were founded in... And we strive to... We have great ambitions to... We think we will change lives... We are passionately interested in humankind... We are backed by all kinds of interesting people... Can we meet so we can bore you some more?'

The first problem with both of these pitches is that when you get to paragraph four – if an investor stays the distance, and it is seriously doubtful that he or she will – they find themselves thinking, 'And the point is?' or, 'What on earth has this got to do with me?'

No one, least of all a busy investor or mentor, has the time to wade through your CV and your five year plan to find out what you want and how it is relevant to him or her. You have to frontload the relevance and the request.

The second problem in these pitches is the six 'I's in the first one and the six 'We's' in the second one. Both pitches are all about the promoter. There is absolutely nothing to attract the investor or even to encourage him or her to keep reading.

How about first telling potential investors or mentors what is in it for them? And why this idea is something they will definitely be interested in, which will fit well with their other interests and which will bring a good return?

Your personal details can be added later as background information. If the idea is a good one that instantly appeals, and it is obviously a fit, the investor may then read on down to find out about the person behind it.

So the email might go something like this instead:

'Hello Michael. I hope you don't mind a direct approach, but I want to tell you about the Wonder Widget because it fits really well with your other products and has the potential to bring you a really good return.

It is at a very interesting stage of development and you might like to hear about it before anyone else, and to consider taking some equity and entering a distribution arrangement when it goes into production later this month.

The margins are exciting and as far as we know, there are no competing products on the market, which will suit your policy of exclusivity. Here is a short outline of the development of the product and the experience of the promoters:'

This letter is all about Michael, the potential investor, not about the promoter. The 'ask' is very clear and upfront. It is business-like and to the point with no faffing about.

The charitable or other type of ask needs to be equally clear, with the detail on the policies and aims of the organisation held to the end for optional reading.

'Hello Michael. The feature on you in this week's Sunday paper caught our attention. You seem to be very interested in sports education for young people and our charity is something that would certainly help you achieve your aims.

As a speaker at our event next March, you would reach your key audience and would be able to impress upon them your concerns in an area that is obviously really close to your heart.

We can't pay a speaker's fee, but would be very happy to cover your expenses on the day. And we would also like to invite you to sit on our board if that is something that would interest you.'

So again the 'ask' is clear, and the fact that it is a charity with no budget, but the plus is obvious – a focused audience and an opportunity to further a cause where there is already a well-established interest.

The aim of a paper pitch is first and foremost that it gets read. The 90 per cent I mentioned above rarely do. And you just know that the promoters are back there at the desk, fuming away at the rudeness of the recipient in not replying, when they should be blaming themselves for approaching it incorrectly in the first place.

And then of course there is the email or telephone request for the dreaded 'cup of coffee'.

The reason investors rarely respond to the 'cup of coffee' request is that it would require leaving the office, driving to the location, having the coffee, listening to something they may have no interest in, and driving back. Thus losing the best part of a morning or an afternoon, which is probably already seriously overloaded, and which would be much better spent working on one of their existing investments.

Lots of start-ups don't seem to understand this. They would be much better advised to write a good pitch, push the correct buttons with an investor or mentor with the correct profile, and they just might get the meeting – and the result – they want.

The Live Pitch

Once upon a time we would get a call from the CEO of a semi-state organisation. After the usual pleasantries were exchanged, he would say he needed a few people trained up. A price was agreed, a few dates put in the diary and we would turn up and deliver the training.

And then after a polite interval we'd send in an invoice and, lo and behold, a cheque would arrive in the post a few days later. It was that simple.

Nowadays, in the interest of fairness and transparency, we all have to go through public tendering with a fully scored and marked decision-making process.

This means that more and more business is won on the basis of the 'beauty parade'; the line-up of businesses who make it through the tendering process called in to a live pitch to demonstrate their credentials and competence. It can be stressful for the pitcher, but it is a great way of allowing the buyer to see how people really perform under pressure.

You can spend lots of time and money preparing the tender document, setting out your stall and proving your competence and experience. But in reality all it is doing is entering you in the competition.

It is a bit like sending in a résumé for a job. Now you have to do the interview, and excel at the interview to win the business.

So here is what you need to know.

A pitch is not a test, it is a date!

You have been invited to pitch on the basis of your document, so you have obviously impressed them with your ability and your knowledge. Now they have to find out if they like you, and if they want to take this exciting new relationship to the next level.

So you need to make your pitch as lively, interesting, relevant and memorable as you know how.

This is not the same thing as reading out the document they already have; or giving a slide presentation of the document they already have; or listing out facts and figures you already very carefully provided them with. It is about:

Energy

Enthusiasm

Engagement

It is about showing them clearly that you know and love their product or service, and are ready and willing to embark on the journey of helping them to achieve their goals. It is about:

Competence

Connection

Completion

It is about starting a real connection where both sides feel this is good for the long haul; and where the work will be delivered to the highest possible standards over the duration of the contract.

De-formalise it

In a classic pitch, the promoter first pitches the idea formally and uninterrupted for a number of minutes, often using visuals. This is followed by a question and answer phase, and then by a negotiation if a deal is on the table. It is very interesting to watch contrasting styles and approaches, and to see how differently people perform throughout the various phases.

There are those who stumble and stutter through the formal phase. But they can settle into it, and some do well when the formal part is over and a real conversation around the product starts, particularly if their knowledge and passion begin to shine through.

The opposite can also happen. You see a really slick, polished initial presentation, but when the investors begin to drill down, it becomes obvious that the promoter has put all his eggs into the presentation basket and has given very little thought to the Q & A or to the negotiation.

The other kind of pitch where formality can really reduce the ability to perform is the kind used on accelerator programmes all over the world. Participants are given a 10-slide template and told to pitch to this format on the Demo Day at the end, when investors are lined-up and the potential for big funding is at stake.

I'm not sure which genius dreamt that one up, but you may as well ask promoters to stick on a straitjacket before they start.

Recently I saw a group on an accelerator programme asked to start preparing their pitches as follows:

110

	THE SLIDES	THE REACTION
SLIDE 1	The name of the company and the promotors	That's us!
SLIDE 2	The problem we solve	That's us again
SLIDE 3	Our product or service	More about us
SLIDE 4	Our market	Yes, you guessed it, more about us!
SLIDE 5	The revenue model	The things that are going to make us money
SLIDE 6	Who is behind the company	Another chance to talk about us
SLIDE 7	Our competition	The people who got there before us
SLIDE 8	Our differentiator	Us again - how brilliant we are!
SLIDE 9	Our request	We would like you to invest in us
SLIDE 10	Questions	*Hmmmm ...*

Now I happen to know, for a fact, that what any self-respecting investor is thinking at this point is: "I don't think so!"

Ten or fifteen of these dreadful pitches at one sitting and he or she is losing the plot, vowing never, ever, to come to this particular demo day again.

For a pitch to connect with an audience, whether the purpose is to make a sale or get investment, the messaging has to start with what is in it for them, not you.

The best way to do that is to leave the straitjacket at home, and to de-formalise the whole exchange, where possible, from the very start, turning it into a conversation with a purpose.

"Most of my pitches have been sales pitches and in those situations, I try to develop a personal relationship with the person opposite", says Patrick Joy, founding Director of Suretank and an Ernst and Young Entrepreneur of the Year, who says he is always looking for the opportunity to get to the heart of the issue.

"My style is to be very open, to make good eye contact, and to be very well prepared. I like to concentrate on what I consider to be the key three or four messages or points that I want to get across, and I make sure that I know my subject inside out.

"A particular pitch that stands out is the one that I gave in Norway in April 2013 to the twenty-strong investment committee of the private equity company that bought two thirds of my company. I was told it was a tour de force and that my passion for the business was what got them so enthusiastic about acquiring it."

Create Rapport

So how do you create rapport? How do you walk into a room full of strangers, and come out an hour later thinking you have just met some new friends? I call it the long lost cousin effect. If you treat someone like your long lost cousin, he will begin to respond like one.

Warmth, friendliness and a genuine interest in others go a long way towards creating this impression. Familiarity does not breed contempt, as the old saying goes, it actually creates bonds and breaks down barriers.

But you are making it very hard if not impossible for yourself to do warm and friendly, if you have first locked yourself into a slide deck that is all about you and your needs.

Creating rapport in a pitch is about getting a conversation going as early as you possibly can; hearing from the other side their issues, needs and concerns and responding empathetically – not heading off at a gallop into a prepared spiel which might have no relevance whatsoever to where they are at.

And the real trick is to have the confidence to do this even when they have invited you in to 'present' to them, and their people have asked your people what AV support you will need, and you arrive to see their board room all set up for a show.

And you know what you do at a show? You sit back and wait to be entertained, you don't participate.

The problem is that buying and selling is a participative process, and the result you want can't possibly happen if half the room is not participating.

People Buy People

Much in the same way as when you are presenting from a stage or a podium, if you want me to listen to you, and to believe in you, I have to be able to see you. And I don't mean that I can't see you because I got a bad seat behind the pillar. I mean I have to see who you are.

In a pitch you are much closer to me – right across the table or at the end of the room. It is a bit more intimate and maybe a bit more daunting for you. But I still have to be able to see you, if you want me to buy from you, or invest in you. So you have to make sure I do.

You have to use the kind of everyday language that shows your personality to best advantage, and you have intrigue me, entertain me and educate me with examples of how you have solved similar problems to mine with previous customers or products.

Give examples and tell stories

Experienced presenters and trainers, people who are in front of rooms full of people every day, always say they prefer a whiteboard or flip-chart to slides, because the movement of walking to the whiteboard, picking up the marker, and beginning to write, takes the eyes and the ears of the room with you. They are all waiting to see what you produce.

Kieron Sparrowhawk, Chairman of MyCognition says, "I love to draw an idea when pitching. A good picture is so much better to get an idea across. And then if it's strong enough, people will 'see' it, and you have them!

"They may even walk around the table and contribute to the drawing, making it 'theirs', meaning they now own part of it and you are in a collaborative process. That's awesome."

Nothing kills a presentation quicker than abstract generalisations, and dense facts and figures that we can't absorb. We crave illustrations and examples to help us understand and remember what was said.

After you leave the room, particularly if several pitches are being heard in succession, what will they remember? What will make yours standout?

The stories you tell... It's that simple.

Stories of real experiences that are relevent to this potential client will keep you in personal memory, make your communication come alive, allow your personality to show, your expertise to shine, and will allow the other side to warm to you and relate to you.

The stepping stones to success are the anecdotes and the examples. They are what win the business.

Mention the money early

Among the hundreds of people I have put through pitch training, there hasn't been one who was comfortable with the idea of bringing their fee, price or charge up early. But funnily enough, I get great reports back from those who have done it and found to their surprise and delight it works well.

Think of the traditional pitch, where you go through the slide show, and finish by asking, 'Any questions?' The first question invariably is, 'And what is all this going to cost us?' So you spend the entire Q & A phase on the back foot, justifying your price and missing out on the opportunity to be talking about benefits.

I have seen highly experienced people in a professional services firm, who charge eye-wateringly large 'masters of the universe' kind of fees, give a great presentation, and then finish by sheepishly slidingly across the table a document in a folder, and mutter lamely something about the fee structure.

So the client opens the folder, starts peering into it, and again begins to query the price and the whole discussion that follows is all about that.

In a good pitch where rapport has been established early and a real conversation is taking place, you can mention your fees as boldly and as baldly as you like, and spend the rest of the encounter illustrating your experience and your commitment to the project.

If the price has been out there in the air for a while, and the conversation has moved on, the questions are more likely to be about the deliverables and there is much less onus on you to defend the number.

Believe me, this works.

And then, don't negotiate the fees until you've secured the business. Only when you have established that you are the preferred supplier should you enter any discussions about reducing the price or offering bulk discounts.

Your price is your price. It is out there, leave it there and focus on the good stuff, kicking to touch any conversation about potential wriggle room until they have said you are in line for the business.

If they can't concede that on the day, well then you can't concede anything on the price. But if they are bringing you back as the lead runner, then you can indicate there might be room for movement.

Pitching as part of a team

A team presentation has a very different dynamic to the individual pitch. It has the advantage of having colleagues along with you who will 'have your back', and mop up any questions you are not comfortable with. But it has the big disadvantage of making you all look 'clunky' and ill at ease if you haven't rehearsed well, and put together a firm strategy for how the pitch will play out on the day.

Here are a few things to remember:

Avoid 'Taxi Presentations'

The team has to look, sound and act like a team – a group of people who are aligned in message and performance, and who actually get on well with one another. The last impression you want to give is of a group who met for the first time in the taxi on the way there!

You really need to meet several times before the pitch to work out this strategy, and to do a few run-throughs. The same effort that goes into writing the proposal document should go into rehearsing for the pitch, giving particular attention to how questions will be answered.

You are not pop-up soldiers

Avoid coming across as a group of individuals, each with their own agenda, popping up in turn to say his or her piece, without any reference to what the others are saying.

You are aiming for a seamless conversation, with everyone sounding as if they are responding spontaneously to the points their own teammates are making, as well as to the questions raised from the other side.

It sounds really stilted when the team leader says: "Thank you Tara, now over to Michael to tell you about our marketing strategy".

After each team member has been invited to introduce him or herself, the team leader should put a relevant question to the first speaker from his own team. "Michael, what do you consider is really relevant for marketing here?", which sounds much more conversational. By starting each section with a question, it immediately sounds more interactive, and encourages the other side to engage throughout the pitch and to ask questions early, rather than waiting until the end.

Everyone speak in the first couple of minutes

It is really important that everyone hears his own voice in the room in the first few minutes, to settle down and feel 'legitimised'. Have you ever been at a meeting where the introductions were done badly, and you are left at the end of the room, unsure of when or whether you are supposed to contribute? It is soul destroying.

No team member should be side-lined in a pitch, left down-stage feeling like they only have a bit part. If everyone speaks early, they are a full part of the pitch, on the balls of their feet, and ready to jump in as required.

Be ready to chip in!

The group dynamic of a team is strengthened by a conversational tone, where the participants practically finish each other's sentences and engage with the potential clients across the table. Strange as this may sound, it is what we do in normal conversation all the time.

Doing it in a pitch looks and sounds natural, and moves it away from the formal, set-piece, pop-up-soldiers, unnatural presentations we have all come to hate.

But be careful not to chip in to come to the rescue of your colleague, or to correct him. There is nothing worse than "What Sean is trying to say is….."

If one team member has spoken for several minutes uninterrupted, and is looking like running out of steam, the team leader should ask him a question to help him stay on track, or move on to the next idea by putting an appropriate question to another team member.

The Q and A

Ask questions back

A pitch is not a one-way street, and you are entitled to ask as many questions as you answer. In fact, have a few good questions ready for the Q and A segment, especially in pitches where, despite your best efforts, you have been locked into a formal first half. If you have succeeded in de-formalising the whole process, you will have been asking questions throughout, and making the whole event interactive.

Get clarification before answering

When the client asks a question, clarify the information they are looking for by saying something like, 'Am I right in thinking you would like to know more about how we propose to deal with security? Great, I'll give you our views on that now, and then I'll ask John to give you a few examples of where it has worked well.'

In doing this you have achieved a few things. You have just 'checked in' with the client, you have made sure your information is correctly targeted, and you have also given your colleague notice to come on in with some examples when you are finished.

Find the concern before giving the answer

If the client asks – "Will this work be carried out by you or other colleagues?" – where is the concern, do you think?

It may be that they believe a second division team will actually be put to work on the contract, after the A team has been drafted in just to make the pitch. Or it may be that they think your company is really too busy to give this project the attention it deserves. Or they are concerned about the depth of your organisation.

Don't rattle off an answer before first finding out what their specific concern is, and then answer appropriately.

AID

Remember Address, Illustrate and Direct from the presentations chapter? Use the technique here as well to take control of the questioning, and steer it towards your strong messages. Every question then becomes a great opportunity to highlight your strengths.

If you don't know, say so

Never spoof the answer to a question. If addressing the issue isn't going to work, and you just don't have the facts to hand, say so.

Not knowing the answer can be turned into a positive. It is a great excuse to get back later with the information that was looked for, which is an opportunity to strengthen the relationship, to thank them again for having you in to pitch, and possibly to get some immediate feedback on how it went.

Ending the Q and A

You can't ask too many questions but sometimes you can be met with silence if you finish the presentation with "Thank you for listening, have you any questions?"

It is often better for the team leader to say "We are coming to the end of our presentation, but before we wrap up we want to make sure we have addressed all the issues. (Address one of the clients specifically, by name). John/Mary have we answered all your concerns about the time frame or is there anything else we can cover now for you in the time we have left?"

If there are still no questions, the team leader can use this opportunity to restate the key differentiators of his team.

The On-the-Spot or Elevator Pitch

New politicians often talk about having the notes for their 'stump' speech in the pocket or handbag at all times. This is the multi-purpose, fits-all-occasions speech that can be whipped out at a moment's notice when called upon to say a few words, topped and tailed to suit the particular event.

The 'after' impression they are aiming for is of someone on top of their game, in control, with a grasp of the facts, ready and willing to deliver results. Whether they achieve that or not is, of course, another story.

For the rest of us, the elevator pitch is similar – a form of words that describes our current project to best advantage, which can be called into good effect should we meet someone influential by chance, well – in the elevator.

The idea is to get vital information out quickly, efficiently and with enough style to impress, and enough of a hook to leave them wanting to know more – all delivered in the time it takes to move between floors.

Anyone running a business, or developing a product or service, needs an elevator pitch for a chance meeting with a financier, a potential backer or an industry expert who might open a few doors.

It is also really useful at the networking events we all seem to attend lately, for telling people what you do, or what problem you solve, quickly and clearly and without boring the pants off them!

'I make these really cool office chairs that look great and will allow you to sit in a better position, reducing back pain. If I was to drop one around to your office this week for you to try out, what colour would you go for?'

In the corporate world, the elevator pitch is a handy tool for reputation enhancement and career advancement. Made to look natural and spontaneous, it is the difference between an awkward silence on the walk from the car park to the front door with senior management, and an opportunity to shine.

'You might like an update on the Benson project, Jennifer? Sales are good and we are delighted with the three new client signings. Actually, now that I think of it, the team would really love your view on the revised marketing strategy. Would you have time to drop down to us later today?'

That sounds smart, focused and interested, and definitely beats mumbling about the weather, or peering at the mobile phone for cover.

Whatever the circumstances, the elevator pitch needs to do a few things. It needs to give a snapshot of the current situation, a sense of progression, and an idea of how things can be in the future. And above all, it needs to be fair and accurate, and not an exaggeration, or it will backfire.

And if you are at that networking event, watch out for a faraway look coming into the eyes of the person you are speaking with. That is your signal to change the subject. They are clearly not interested in your beautiful ergonomic chairs, so connect on a personal level instead, and talk about the football.

∝

All the points above have been developed through working with hundreds of companies and individuals over the years on pitch training, and then getting feedback afterwards; hearing great stories of deals won, contracts signed and investment achieved.

But it is only theory until you put it into practice. So you need to rehearse yourself and your team prior to a big pitch until you are so comfortable with the material that you can focus your full attention on the other side – and work out what is really going on in the room at all times, so you can adapt accordingly.

Chapter Six

Meetings That Make Sense

In this chapter, you will hear about the things that make meetings work, and also about the things that make them falter, fizzle out and completely waste everyone's time! And there is also a full run down on how to become a really efficient and high performing Chairperson, or meeting organiser.

You know this person: the kind of guy lots of people want to be. He is a very good looking 55 and keeps himself really trim and fit. He runs a great business, has a beautiful home, an amazing wife and family and drives a fast car.

Out socialising, he is the life and soul of the party. You could bring him anywhere, and as a friend, he's the very best.

The problem is that I can't stand to be in a meeting that he chairs, and neither can most of the other people around the table.

We had occasion some years back to serve on the same board, where he had been elected Chair, and I began to dread the meetings, knowing that they would be a nightmare of late starts, indecision, rambling thoughts, long-winded statements, and absolutely no direction given to anyone or anything.

As the board got into the swing of its lifespan, I took him aside and gently pointed out that people had lives and homes to go to, and that really we should try to keep the meetings to an hour in length, or an hour and a half at a push. The previous month, the meeting had run for three hours, and by the end of it people were seriously disgruntled.

He heard me out with grace and acceptance of well-intentioned feedback, and then proceeded to let the meeting run for three hours all over again. This time the participants were fulminating as they left for home, and threatening all kinds of dire consequences on his head, which he was and remains to this day blissfully unaware of.

Because he mistakenly thinks that he is doing a great job; that the lovely affable personality he is blessed with, and which is great on the social scene, works just as well in the boardroom.

> *He thinks* that starting a meeting at 10.20 as opposed to 10am is just giving people space to hang their coats, get coffee and socialise for a bit.

> *He thinks* that chatting away until 10.40 is opening the meeting in a relaxed way, with plenty of time to reflect on last month's activities.

> *He thinks* that allowing people to ramble on without summarising, or noting action points, is giving them space to express themselves.

He thinks that asking every person there to re-cap on all they have been doing, whether they have anything to say or not, is fair and equitable, when he should be seeing that pertinent issues drive the agenda.

He thinks that the clock is a wall decoration.

As you sit there, with the time going on and a thousand things to be done back at the desk or at home, and you have to listen to someone make up a report which is no different to the one they gave last month, you start planning your resignation from the board.

A Chair's first responsibility is to use the meeting as a touchpoint to keep the team focused, aligned, moving forward and above all believing in the project and the potential outcomes. A poorly run meeting will put everyone in a bad mood, and halve productivity for the rest of the day.

As an attendee at a meeting you have different responsibilities – to prepare well, to report clearly, to make evidence-based contributions, and to hear what others are saying, and we'll come to that shortly.

But let's look at Chairing first, an opportunity to really perform, or to crash and burn, like my friend above.

Chairing a Meeting

There are four 'must haves' for a well-run meeting:

1. Time Constraints

2. Good Preparation

3. Solid Presentations

4. A Chair who is in control

Time Constraints

We are all busy with a hundred things to fit into our day, so we want to know when the meeting is going to start, and equally when it is going to end. So it is important to state clearly on the agenda the start and finish times. How many meeting notifications have you received with a start time, and nothing at all about how long each item is going to take, or when you might get out of there?

My gym starts classes at 9.25am or 6.10pm – the offbeat time makes you remember it and turn up on time. So there is a theory that if you say the meeting is at 2pm, participants may straggle in at 2.05 or 2.10, whereas if you call the meeting for 2.10 in the first place, they might be there on time.

Worth a try, but I'd be inclined to call the meeting for 1.45 arrival and coffee, saying it will kick off at 2pm sharp. But then you have to follow through and start at 2pm on the button, so that those who are late miss the top of the meeting and make a better effort to be there next time.

No point in rewarding the latecomers by waiting for them, and punishing those on time by leaving them sitting around!

Another good idea is to have the time you are allocating for each item on the agenda clearly stated; ten minutes for item four, fifteen minutes for item seven and so on. Deadlines make people reach decisions, and a strong Chair with an eye on the clock reminds people that the time for that particular item is coming to a close. So people make their minds up, and the meeting is more productive.

Preparation

As the Chair, you need to prepare well for the meeting. Draw up your agenda, with the timings attached, and circulate it a number of days beforehand. Seems obvious, but it is amazing how few Chairs actually do it.

The agenda should include the specific issues and the clear-cut objectives to be addressed, with a note attached to each agenda item on what the aim is – a discussion, an information piece, a decision, or a recommendation to the executive. The board works much better if they know exactly what is expected of them.

If you want any of the attendees to deliver a presentation, or to provide a written response for the meeting, state clearly what duration or length is required and what format the input is to take.

Presentations or Reports

It is up to the Chair to see that contributing participants plan their piece well, and understand to deliver it in a clear and interesting manner within the prescribed time. Ideally you should contact them in advance, to firstly ask them to make the contribution, but then to brief them on exactly what you want from the item.

So you might say:

"We don't like being talked at, and we are quite informal, so no need for power point, or to feel you have to pump the facts at us. We would much prefer a conversation around the issue, and to hear your insights, with the facts and figures on a sheet that we can look at afterwards. How does that sound?"

or

"I'd like a short presentation from you – no longer than 5 minutes – giving an overview of the situation, but then you need to be prepared to take questions for 15 or 20 minutes. They are a very interactive board and will want to get to the heart of how this came about. But don't worry, they are looking forward to meeting you, and know that what you have to say will be really interesting and relevant."

So you are doing two things here as Chair – you are setting up the presenter to contribute well, and you are 'producing' your meeting, making sure that things will be relevant and interesting for everyone there.

A Chair who is in control

A good Chair is clearly on top of the material, has briefed people well, has an obvious plan, communicates it well to all present and runs the meeting efficiently and well.

Tom Savage was my Chairman on the Board of RTÉ, the Irish National Broadcaster, where I served for five years and I personally really enjoyed his style. He had a talent for making each person in the room feel that the words they had just uttered were the most important thing that had been said that day. But then to move rapidly on to the next item, before you lost the run of yourself entirely!

As a State board, there was also the luxury of a very strong secretariat, so the board pack and agenda arrived like clockwork three or four days before the monthly meeting, allowing you plenty of time to do your reading and prepare for the meeting.

But if I was to pick out the key things that I have noted good Chairs do, over many years of observing them – and trying to be one myself – it is that:

- They open the meeting very pointedly at the specific time, welcoming the participants and thanking them for their attendance. And they remind participants the time at which the meeting will be concluding.

- They state the goals and specific objectives of the meeting; what's for discussion, what is to be decided, and what is to be actioned.

- At the start of each agenda item, they make a 30-60 second opening statement on the item and solicit quick views from around the room, before the item is discussed in depth.

- They never go around the room in order of seating, saying: "We'll start with you Pat and go round this way and hear everyone's views." They know that it is better to hop around, keeping everyone awake and on their toes.

- They never allow two people to talk at once, or for side-bar conversations to emerge, and they never discuss anything but the item at this point on the agenda.

- They announce the speaker they are going to come to after the next speaker, to allow that person set themselves up. For example, "I'll come to Claire after Hilary. Hilary do you agree with what Colm said?"

- They make it clear that they are winding up the discussion on this item very shortly, and they keep mentioning the magic word "decision". For example, "Ok, have we any final views before we make our decision, and go on to the report from the Sales Division?"

- They feel consensus emerging, and move quickly for a decision. They say things like: "Ok, I am keen to move on because I want to allow ample time to hear the updates from Colin about the project and we also have to hear from Jacinta about the exhibition".

- They compliment those who make concise contributions, rather than criticising those who talk too much. They know that positive reinforcement gets results.

- They sit back and allow those who wish to express an opinion do so, before coming in with one of their own. They know not to enter into dialogue, as this can dilute the authority of their chairmanship.

- They take notes, specifically when decisions have been reached, drawing attention to the fact that the decision has been taken and noted, and the item closed.

- They only call for a vote as a last resort. They know that it can be divisive, and use it sparingly as a means of wrapping something up.

- They never let a meeting fizzle out at the end or splutter to a close. With 10 minutes to go, they remind everyone that they plan on finishing at the agreed time, as per the agenda, and they call for a wrap-up on the last item and any other business.

- They make a one-minute closing statement including a brief reminder of decisions taken, a mention of important follow-up actions to be undertaken, including deadlines, and they thank participants and end the meeting formally and authoritatively.

If you can remember to do most of these things stylishly and well at important meetings you chair, add in some humour and a genuine interest in people, you will be a good leader and teams will enjoy your meetings.

Is This Meeting Really Necessary?

Did you spot the key words in the last paragraph? They were 'important meetings'. I am hugely mindful of the fact that years worth of human lives are being wasted, right at this very moment, in offices and concerns all over the world at lengthy, pointless and meaningless meetings.

There are meetings to set up meetings and meetings to discuss previous meetings and meetings to discuss future meetings. And people 'sitting in' on meetings and 'observing' meetings and referencing meetings, and minuting meetings.

And you would sometimes wonder what it is all for, or what is the real objective with any of them?

So before you rush to call a meeting, or several meetings, to try out the chairmanship skills we have been discussing, you have to ask yourself a few questions:

- Is a meeting at this point the only way to fulfil my objectives?

- Is a meeting the BEST way to fulfil my objectives?

- What are the alternatives?

- Will a meeting use my time and my colleagues' time to our best advantage?

- Is this meeting only being held because it's Friday and that's what we do   on Fridays?

- Could an email, with several key questions, get a quicker and clearer result?

- Could a conference call get the same result?

If you decide that face time and a full meeting is absolutely essential to move the project along, you now have to decide who needs to be at the meeting. The fewer the better is probably a good rule of thumb – the duration of the meeting directly proportionate to the number of people attending.

So you do have to consider who are you obliged to invite to this meeting? As in, who can cause trouble if not invited? Or who will be an ally and give you what you want? You need to think about who will be in favour of your objective, who will oppose it and who will sit firmly on the fence?

So now send out a memo of invitation. If you are absolutely sure that this meeting needs to take place, then take it seriously and structure it to get the results you want.

The memo gets the meeting into people's diaries and confirmed well before time. It makes people realise that they have to show up and bring something to the picnic. And it is a good way of communicating effectively, even where you are not an official Chair and cannot assume that title.

The alternative – "Why don't you and the team drop into my office at 4pm" – is more casual, and people will take that meeting as relaxed and not requiring any special preparation.

Understanding the Meeting Dynamic

No matter where they take place, or in what language they are conducted, all meetings follow a particular pattern.

No matter where they take place, or in what language they are conducted, I think you'll agree that all meetings follow a particular pattern. Someone states a case. Others support or argue against that case. Someone then proposes an alternative case or cases, and alliances begin to be formed for those new cases or for the original one. Then a bit of movement starts to happen, and people may change position, a decision becoming clear and agreement reached and minuted.

To get your proposals over the line you need to understand the meeting dynamic and the value of timing; you have to spot movement, and you may well need to have acquired some allies before the day.

If you have one or two people teed up to support your proposal before it has ever come up, you are half-way there.

It is said that most board decisions are actually made in the corridor outside the boardroom, or on the golf course the day before. I don't play golf, so I can't confirm that one, but I can appreciate where the phrase 'corridors of power' originates. I do know that strategic alliances are formed well in advance of a big meeting, and the decisions in the room are often a foregone conclusion.

Let's just call it office politics – not a dirty word, as some people think, but simply an understanding of the sources and uses of power.

When we are working with groups on meeting skills we do an exercise that really demonstrates how this works. I have seen senior partners in law and accountancy firms enter the role play with gusto, and really enjoy the results.

We give the group a topic to discuss, something out of the normal course of business so they can really let their hair down. The topic might be, for example, that we are redecorating this board room; what style should we go for and how much should we spend on it. Then we give 'stances' to the participants, which their colleagues are not party to. So Dearbhla is hell-bent on a blue boardroom, John wants yellow, Peter doesn't give a toss what colour it is as long as John doesn't get his own way, Grainne wants to spend nothing, thinks it is fine as it is, and so on.

The exercise is to see who gets their own way, and the funny part, for us as trainers, is that we can always predict with a complete certainty who that will be! Because all meetings follow a pattern, and once you know the pattern, you are far more likely to achieve your goal.

In meeting skills training programmes, I talk to people about the:

Shut up

Sit up

Tot up

Put up

Mop up

method of working a meeting to your advantage.

Shut Up is first and it is surprising to many to learn that those who talk the least, particularly at the start of a meeting, can influence the most. Too often we land into a meeting bursting with the brilliance of our great information and dying to throw it all on the table.

But this is when resistance is at its highest and the best of ideas can get lost because positions are adopted before people fully understand the concepts - positions they can't go back on later without losing face.

Often it is not what you say or how much you say that carries the day in a crucial meeting. It is all about when you make your case. People who stay quiet and listen can work out exactly where others are coming from and get their timing right.

Sit Up comes next. This is where you pay close attention to what is being said, asking questions for clarity, and noting from the body language, exchanged glances, and other non verbal signals who is aligned with whom.

Tot Up is where you start to see who is for and against the proposal on the table, and who may be aligned with yours when you land it. There will be those at the table who are against the current proposal, because they are against the person who made it, and who will gladly support an alternative. Any alternative. Particularly when things have been going around for a while and fresh thinking is clearly needed.

Put Up You feel the movement, and you put your proposal up on the table fast. Your timing is right, people will go for it, and you can start to bring it home.

Mop Up "Well it seems we have some consensus there so will we take that as a decision? Great, we can move on then to the finance report." And guess what? You are home and hosed. Your proposal has just been carried.

To sum up, all meetings have three phases, or three phases for each agenda item.

The Presentation phase –
When participants set out their stalls

The Positioning phase –
When participants check out the lie of the land

The Movement phase –
When consensus begins to emerge.

The challenge is in staying on your toes while the first two phases are underway, so that you are fully alert to when the movement phase starts, and poised to seize the moment.

But don't let it drag on. As soon as you have the bones of an agreement grab it, verbalise it, note it and confirm it back to the meeting straight away.

Participating rather than Chairing or Organising

As an active participant in a meeting, you will have to prepare properly if you want your contribution to mean anything and to resonate. It's true you won't have the same onus to keep the show on the road as the Chair or Organiser, but you have a personal responsibility not to waffle either.

You will know from attending unproductive meetings that the ones that go pear-shaped usually have:

- No specific objectives for the meeting, its leader or its participants

- No agenda set or circulated in advance.

- Too many participants or the wrong participants

- Unprepared participants

- Participants with no understanding of the politics

- Contributors who talk too much

- Contributors who inflict Death by PowerPoint on their colleagues

- Too many digressions and interruptions.

- Time wasted on "Why" rather than "How".

- Mixed final decisions due to lack of closure and weak chairing

We can blame poor chairmanship for lots of this but we can also blame poor participation. To become an effective contributor to meaningful meetings, you should make a decision, right now, that you will never 'sit in' on a meeting again.

Your time is far too valuable.

You will only attend a meeting with a very specific objective in mind – to hear something, to learn something, to contribute something or to influence an outcome.

You are not a spectator and you have to know why you are there and what you hope to get out of the experience.

Ask yourself, why are you at this meeting? How are you going to contribute to this meeting? What do you want to achieve following the meeting?

If you have been asked to contribute background information for an agenda item, particularly when reporting up to the board, prepare your report to the time slot allowed, keeping it simple and interesting.

Non-executive directors come from a wide variety of backgrounds, and while they may be very experienced in corporate governance they may actually know little about the technical side of the business.

Don't blind them with science or use industry jargon which they won't embarrass themselves by asking you to explain. Keep your presentation in simple language, and use plenty of examples to illustrate what you are saying.

And front load your information! Don't keep the good stuff till last and don't make the board work to find out what you are on about. You are supposed to cut through all the detail, and bring clarity and insight. That is why you are there.

One time on the board of a national concern, we got a complex report from a senior member of the team with an executive summary that had about three lines, more or less saying – you asked for this report, here it is, there are loads of findings in there, go and root for them yourself.

The report was lengthy and part of a huge board pack that had come out that month. As I was settling down on the sofa with a heavy sigh to tackle into it, my daughter said to me 'You are going to need chocolate with that one, Mam'.

She was right!

Meetings are a necessary evil for most of us, taking up far more of our time than we perhaps like. But with some thought and preparation, they can be interesting, productive, and even enjoyable.

And don't forget they are a brilliant touch-point for catching up with colleagues, and for having those side-bar conversations – both personal and business – that can lead on to so much.

As a lively, engaged and well prepared Chair or contributor, you can make the whole experience better for yourself and your colleagues, and get the results you want efficiently and quickly.

Chaper Seven

Negotiating Successfully

*In this chapter we look at closing the odds when
it comes to achieving our goals in a negotiation,
something I heard defined beautifully by a
colleague as 'the art of achieving wise outcomes'.*

Going into a tense negotiation is the modern day version
of going into battle.

We arm ourselves with all the facts and figures,
sharpen the saw with strong self-talk, gather up the team
and motivate them well, choose the location for the bout,
apply the war-paint, and head on over the hill hoping we
are smarter, faster or more agile than the other side.

But of course it isn't a battle, and there shouldn't
be winners or losers. The strongest negotiations are
based on a collaborative model – an understanding from
both sides that the goal is solving a shared problem, and
reaching that outcome in a dignified and respectful way.

On a breakfast TV panel one time, we were
discussing the proposed purchase of the Irish
government's shareholding in Aer Lingus by AIG,

and I made the point that the staff were central to the negotiations; that without their buy-in, any change in control would be slower and more cumbersome.

Another panellist, a newspaper journalist, asked me where I got my quaint notions from. He said the staff were totally unimportant to the negotiations, the only thing that mattered was the politics involved.

And that is exactly where negotiations crash and burn.

Just as well the gentleman in question is a good journalist, because he will never be a manager, or a negotiator. If those on either side of a divide actually feel that the people in an organisation are unimportant, and let those feelings be known, the thing is doomed before it even starts.

Negotiations are conducted by people, about people, for an outcome that is going to affect people. Yes, things like the politics, and the stocks and shares, and who is ultimately going to pay the bill, are hugely relevant and important.

But on the day, around the table, it is people who will do the talking, and ultimately find resolution or not, depending on their own attitude and preparedness.

If you want to become a good negotiator, a good place to start is probably with the realisation that you have been negotiating successfully every day, all your life, and others have been negotiating equally successfully with you.

You negotiated a loan to buy your house; with your neighbour to stop parking his car in front of your gate; with your partner to go away for the weekend with the team; with your best friend to return – eventually – the hair-dryer she borrowed.

Your kids have been negotiating successfully with you, since forever, for extra time on the X-box, more pocket money, an extra hour out playing on a bright night, a later curfew during half-term and so on. And they are darn good at it.

They marshal the facts, present them well, add in a bit of emotional blackmail, give you those eyes, the killer smile, and the job is done.

So negotiating is an activity we are well practised at, and one that is relatively simple when the stakes are low and the outcome is not earth shattering. It gets tougher when the bar is higher and the outcome is going to seriously affect you or those you are responsible for.

Failed negotiations can lead to loss of money or jobs, businesses closing, relationships breaking down, de-motivated teams and lots of other disastrous consequences.

I believe that a successful negotiation has to start with respect for the other side and with a genuine desire to play the ball and not the person. The other side is not an enemy, an opponent or an adversary. You are not heading into a game of rugby where the heaviest pack will gain the inches. It is not about bulldozing, besting or bullying people.

It is about doing the homework, being very clear on needs, presenting the strongest case you can, listening well, understanding your BATNA – more about that below - and, as the song goes, knowing when to hold and knowing when to fold.

As the founding fathers of modern negotiation, Roger Fisher and William Ury put it:

"The reason you negotiate is to produce something better than the results you can obtain without negotiating. What are those results? What is that alternative? What is your **BATNA** – your Best Alternative To a Negotiated Agreement? That is the standard against which any proposed agreement should be measured."

Start with the Homework

Good research is key to the success of any negotiation, something that is easier than ever to accomplish. So there is no excuse. You can find out lots about the other side on websites, social and traditional media, and through having discussions with key people – remembering through which particular prism the view is coming.

The company website and their published material = their view

Newspaper and online coverage = a moderated (journalist's) view

What is said on social media = external (perhaps uninformed) view

Former employees = external (perhaps disgruntled) view

Strategic partner = internal (probably informed) view

Site or plant visit = bird's eye view

Current employees = internal (ground up) view

Current management = internal (top down) view

This kind of research will yield some really good perspective on the other side and hopefully on the team they will be fielding on the day. Knowing and understanding past form of the players is very helpful, and any insight to their background, experience and drivers will inform how you approach the meeting.

A reach out before the event is always good – some personal contact that begins to establish rapport and a degree of trust – also some agreement on the agenda, if possible, and ground rules.

Social media is one way to reach out informally. Favouriting and sharing other people's posts is a great way of showing you care. We are all flattered by it.

But it's not enough on its own. It should be followed by a formal email or a good old fashioned telephone conversation to break the ice and reinforce the notion that the problem will be put on the table, and discussed dispassionately, with the objective of finding a workable resolution for all.

Unplanned negotiations take a different kind of preparation, more of a mental preparedness, and an agility that allows you see all the options and go down all the avenues.

Scott McDonald is the CEO of Noise Solutions Inc, based in Alberta, Canada. In 2009, when the world economy went pear-shaped, he had to hold his nerve in the face of illness and the banks playing hardball. He told me he had to respond really quickly to negotiate the terms with stakeholders that would allow his business to survive.

"We had expanded our company to include US sales teams – our first real boots on the ground in the US

– and sales were expanding like crazy. Our revenue in the US went from 10 per cent to 55 per cent of our global sales. We looked like superstars.

"Then the world economy collapsed, and our sales simply dried up, and the US fell to between 2–3 per cent of our revenues. Oh, and this all happened while I was in bed for 12 days with the H1N1 virus and unaware of the situation.

"When I awoke, I found my company in crisis, my business partner checked out of the business and staff wondering what the hell was going to happen.

Then my bank called a $2.5 million loan due in 30 days.

"I negotiated a 90-day extension on the loan – why do banks always charge you more money when you have none? I worked on refinancing all of my plant property and equipment, hired a CFO, and negotiated quicker pay terms from my existing clients. One client found out about our situation and paid out $1.5 million in less than 24 hours.

"We had to downsize the company and temporarily reduce staff and salaries by over 60 per cent, through wage reduction and layoffs, 120 staff to 40. This bought us the time needed to wait through the economic blip and enter the new world economy. I have never had a demand loan since."

Through reacting quickly, negotiating well and listening to the ideas from his core team, Scott turned his business around and within a few years had built it right back up.

Choosing the team

We all have characteristic communication styles under pressure and an awareness of these is crucial before going into a negotiation. The people you need to strenuously avoid bringing onto your negotiating team are:

The Commander

This one is the Boss, and has the sign on the door to prove it. Very often an alpha personality, he or she may have spent too much time in dressing-rooms listening to pep talks along the lines of 'make every blow a wound'.

Mistakenly, they think that the game is about letting the other side know, at every opportunity, that they are losing. They play 'dirty' before, during and after the negotiation.

He doesn't give the other side a chance to prepare properly, and during the meeting may use threatening language, make personal remarks, demand impossible concessions, or use every available opportunity to upset the other side.

The Commander thinks that this is being powerful; a 'don't mess with me' kind of negotiator.

The Contrarian

This one has a fixed position, at extreme odds with the other side, and thinks that holding the line at all costs is what it is about. She takes no responsibility for the outcome, finding satisfaction in withstanding each and every perceived attack on her stance.

There is only one result, as far as this one is concerned, the complete and total about face of the opposition, and the acknowledgement that they were right all along.

The Calamatist

This one sees danger and adversity everywhere. *There be monsters out there!* His nervousness and unease as he steps through the door for the negotiation is palpable and noted by everyone in the room. It doesn't matter what words he uses now, his body language has already said it all.

As the meeting progresses, he may overreact to what is said, he may blurt out assertions rather than cite facts, he may become emotive. He may not have his brain in gear.

The Circumventor

This one is a straw in the wind, and is so anxious for a resolution, any resolution, that she comes across as weak and indecisive.

She doesn't have a BATNA, makes concessions too easily, tries one thing and then another, and is absolutely terrified of deadlock.

She too takes no responsibility for the outcome, and afterwards will blame all kinds of external circumstances for the lack of a result.

The Player

The wing men and women you need with you on the day of a crucial negotiation know all those characters above, and know to never show up that way themselves!

Good team members are willing to do good

research, resilient and focused, capable of listening as much as talking and flexible and willing to compromise.

And they know to leave personal feelings outside the door, leave judgemental and critical language at home, manage their non verbal signals and communicate clearly and directly

Those are the team members who will have your back, who will be mindful and present, and who will be a real asset on the day.

Planning the Strategy

Earlier I quoted Roger Fisher and William Ury. Their seminal book *Getting to Yes* has been on the business best-seller list for years. Their central premise is that you always had to leave something for the other side; if you allow everyone gain some small thing, a negotiation has every chance of concluding satisfactorily.

In series three of *House of Cards*, US President Frank Underwood and Russian President Petrov are in the Kremlin negotiating late into the night on a wide ranging deal covering US involvement in the Middle East. In the earlier away game, from the Russian perspective, Petrov had been firmly in Commander mode, as described earlier, but now on the home leg, he has softened somewhat and seems more open to movement.

Underwood, spotting his opportunity, moves into classic *Getting to Yes* territory, and says: 'Why don't we start mapping out what a potential agreement might look like?"

So in this example they haven't reached agreement yet; they are not even close, but just for the exercise, a good negotiator is suggesting that they park the objections for the moment and start talking about what possible common ground might look like.

By doing this, each side inevitably start being more favourably disposed towards each other, and starts using the language of agreement, which might even lead to real agreement. It is spotting the opportunity, and moving in.

Your strategy planning session should start with your **BATNA** – the Best Alternative to a Negotiated Agreement – which ultimately protects you from accepting terms that are too unfavourable to you, and from rejecting terms that might be in your interest to accept. Having a good understanding of this hugely increases your negotiating power.

You work out your **BATNA** based on defining issues and problems – not people or emotions; interests and genuine needs – not positions or stances.

And then you get really creative, and start working on places where you can find, suggest, or invent mutual gain.

And you use evidence, facts and history to platform these places, not generalisations, or feelings, or bias.

Your strategy also needs to take into account a whole bunch of what ifs:

What if the proposed agreement is better than our **BATNA**? Accept it

What if the proposal is worse than our **BATNA**? Keep negotiating

What if they will not move? Start listing options for mutual gain

What if there is absolute deadlock? Can each side attain small goals in a distributive way?

What if you are coming to the end of the line? Take a break and try again

Walking the Walk

Success in negotiation is very much about anticipation – working out what the other side might do, how they might behave on the day, and preparing accordingly.

Here are some of the situations you might encounter:

Difficult or intransigent people: Need to be spotted early and disarmed, usually by giving their inputs plenty of attention, and reflecting back to them what they are saying, so that they know you are listening. A good opening phrase is, "I hear you say ..."

"John, I hear you say that you have serious concerns about the Cork operation, and that you have regard for the long serving staff there. I think we share those concerns. I would like to suggest......" and go on to make your point.

Another good move is to clarify the concern before answering a question. So John asks a straight question: "What are you suggesting we do about the Cork operation?"

You reply: "Sure, happy to discuss Cork next, but can I ask you John, for clarity, where are your specific concerns in that regard?"

The chances are, he will explain his concerns – the staff, or the costs, or the media response, or whatever it might be. And then your answer becomes much more focused.

We all love to explain things. We all love being put into the position of 'expert'. We enjoy being asked for advice, and being given the floor to expand. It is very hard to fight when you are listened to attentively, and those around you are sitting up, paying attention, nodding, obviously very interested. It is seriously disarming.

Hidden agendas Asking for clarity is your main tool here. The best negotiators listen twice as much as they talk, and the listening follows carefully posed questions, phrased softly.

"Just so I am absolutely clear here, would you mind explaining the background to that?"

"I know you have probably been over this many times, but for the benefit of my team here, could you give us a synopsis of the situation to date?"

"Am I right in thinking that this point is very central for you? Could you explain why?"

"You have mentioned several concerns. Could I ask you to prioritise those concerns in order of importance to you?"

Aggression It takes two to start a fight and there will never be a row if you do not rise to the bait, regardless of what is said. You have to think of pantomime players going 'oh yes you did', 'oh no you didn't', 'oh yes you did', 'oh no you didn't'; the pitch and tone getting higher and louder, the pace getting faster and faster.

This is a negotiation falling apart.

"Yes, but…" is a much better response than a flat "No", which begs for immediate counter disagreement. Even when you disagree vehemently with the other side, it is better not to say so baldly, as it brings the language of disagreement centre stage.

You should instead be working to allow the language of agreement to flourish. So instead of risking starting a row, you say: "I completely understand why you hold that view, but I'd like to explain my point of view."

Or you could say: "That's one way of looking at it, certainly, but could we now take a few minutes to look at it this way?"

The language in these examples is gentle, even conciliatory, but don't ever confuse that with weakness. It is actually a strength.

Deadlock Giving away minor points in the hope of making a major one can be effective, conceding things that you have found out – by listening – are important to the other side, but not so huge to you. Movement is infectious. Give a little and they will too.

But know that movement is only spotted by those who are open to it. People who are locked into remembering a rehearsed position are using up all their brain's RAM with downloading material from sequential memory. They risk missing what is actually going on in the room.

Those who are fully present, and who are responding intuitively, are freeing up loads of megabytes to watch, feel, listen, observe, and take in everything that is really going on, as well as actually presenting their case.

Walk Outs You have to walk away, regretfully, when despite being mindful of all of the above, the other side is persistently obstructionist, blocking your every move, resisting every suggestion, and clearly not willing or able to work towards a resolution.

And this is where the BATNA is again invaluable. You went into the room hoping for a good resolution, but knowing that you had an alternative if all failed.

But going on the basis that every single thing is negotiable, the walk away, of itself, can be an opportunity for further negotiation – unless you really, really want to slam the door to make a big point!

There is far more to be gained by defusing the tension, as the meeting ends, to allow the possibility of resuming in a few days when people have had time to think, or positions have shifted.

You might say: "So we are clearly not going to reach agreement today, but before we leave, can we discuss some options on how we might resume discussions in time?"

If options can be listed, and discussed, there is a possibility that the best option can be converted into a genuine alternative.

There is a major retail group which conducts its business along, let's say, old fashioned lines. Becoming a buyer there is a legendary training ground, and working on the shop floor fairly testing. If you can survive the jumped up managers in cheap suits, and the regular public dressing downs they love to mete out, you can survive anything.

A client of ours who provides insurance to the company described the negotiations they have once a year to get the repeat business.

"You would wonder what century they think they are in", he says. "In the middle of every negotiation they storm out in a flurry, which we now know after a number of years of doing business with them, is a complete stunt.

"We have stopped getting stressed by it. We just pour some more tea for ourselves, eat a few more chocolate biscuits, and wait for them to come back."

An Early Win So much preparation goes into a negotiation, particularly one carrying a lot of tension, there is a danger that the negotiators will miss an early win by a country mile, and talk themselves right out of it again.

Have you ever listened to a sales pitch, and decided within a minute or two that you are buying the product, only to notice that the sales person hasn't spotted the 'buy' decision on your face, and is carrying right on with the prepared spiel?

You gently interject that yes, you are quite interested in the photocopier or the flat screen, but he keeps going right along, now in full flight, loving the sound of his own voice and the wonderfully learned off and rehearsed pitch? He is happily talking himself out of the sale.

In the same way in a negotiation you approach prepped and armed to the hilt, you might be surprised by an early concession, negating the need to carry on with all your good material.

It's hard to let the good stuff go but it has to be done. You have to fold up the tent, acknowledge the win – with respect and gratitude – and move on.

I was working with a man in a senior role in a technology firm who was going for a major promotion that would have seen him reporting directly to the CEO. The company took the process very seriously and put him through about five rounds of really tense interviewing, involving the international board and other stakeholders.

For every phase of the process, my client put in huge amounts of work, coming through with flying colours, even if it felt like doing a few bouts with a prize fighter. Then it came to the final round when he had to present to the CEO and we worked hard on a great presentation concentrating solely on his vision for the role.

He arrived into the office of the CEO, laptop under his arm, fired up to do the best song and dance act of his life, and the CEO shook his hand and said: "Congratulations, I know you are going to do a great job. Will we go and have a spot of lunch?"

My client said it took a fair few minutes for him to close his mouth and to move on from the reality that his whizz, bang, wallop presentation was not required, and to enjoy the lunch that followed along with a relaxed and very general conversation with the CEO.

Choosing the Location

The big question is, does playing at home give you an advantage and does playing away hamper you? Of course the answer is yes to both. But the choice of location for a tense negotiation is not always yours to make, so you have to make do with what you have.

When I work with clients preparing for a radio or television interview, I remind them that they know their story inside out and back to front, as they speak about this stuff every day, but the environment they will be in is strange and new and that can affect how they perform when the red light goes on.

The interviewer at the other side of the TV studio or radio desk is in his or her living room, that warm cosy place they go every day to do a job they love, surrounded by pleasant colleagues and friends. It is a huge advantage.

You can't move the furniture or sit in a different place in a broadcast studio, but you most certainly can, and probably should, when you arrive at the negotiation venue. Feeling comfortable and in full sight of the room is very important, so you should make it your business to arrive early and get things set up in a way that will work for you.

If a neutral venue is a possibility, go for it. Firstly it levels the playing field but it also offers a better opportunity to do a recce the day before, and get comfortable with the space and how your voice sounds in the room.

During the Negotiation

The best negotiations happen when both sides understand the principles and best practices we have been discussing here, but life, as we know, is not always like that. All we can do is hope that, during the reach-out prior to the negotiation, you have indicated how you intend to proceed, and that the other side will reciprocate with the same degree of civility and respect.

Usually wise outcomes are achieved when both sides have prepared well for the negotiation and have done their homework. If there is collaboration on an agenda, rather than one side or other trying to impose one, things start off well. A neutral venue always helps too, so neither side is playing a home or away match!

So too does clear communication before, during and after the event, along with a level of trust and respect that allows emotions to be kept separate from issues, and problems from personalities. A willingness to note and appreciate small gains is also crucial, I believe, and a chair or mediator who controls things well.

After the Negotiation

When you speak to negotiators about what didn't work in any exchange, they usually come back with the same things. Typically the list includes lack of courtesy, people who are unreasonable in their approach, or stances that were just too far apart to bridge.

Conor Ronan, the CEO of Ronan Group Renewables agrees that the ideal in any negotiation is to go in with an open mind, and to try to leave something behind for the other guy, while actively working on achieving your own goals.

But sometimes despite your best intentions, you are up against a hard-ball attitude from the other side from the outset, which leaves you no option but to respond in kind.

"In a recent deal I was working on, with a Project Capex of €150,000,000, the law firm on the other side came at us like a runaway train, demanding the kitchen sink. We held our ground, and we walked away with the kitchen sink and a few gold taps as well!

"It was very tense during the negotiation, and at one point we thought the whole deal might collapse, but it worked out well for us in the end."

The most common reasons for a negotiation breaking down and falling flat on its face include a lack of clarity about what was really going on in the room; there were lots of words spoken but very little meaning.

Tension, before things even get started, can cripple outcomes, as can posturing and game playing; or poor chairing or mediation. People who get heated, and overly personal in their response to suggestions, can ruin things for everyone; as can people who use deflection and avoidance, or those who try to apportion blame.

At the end of the day negotiating is probably more about getting the other person to talk, than doing the talking yourself. By showing up to a negotiation in a really positive, mindful way, relaxed in the knowledge that you have the work done, you stand to gain so much more through respectfully listening to, and acknowledging, the concerns of the other side.

This attitude will reflect strongly in your body language from the moment you walk through the door, and do more to influence the outcomes than many of the words spoken.

A friendly, attentive, pleasant, and interested demeanour does wonders to set the tone for everything that ensues, as opposed to clenched jaws, squared shoulders, and stony expressions.

Patrick Joy, founding Director of Suretank, and an Ernst and Young Irish Entrepreneur of the Year, told me how, in the best deal of his career, both sides felt they came out well in the end, despite how difficult the negotiations became half way through.

"It was the sale of 67 per cent of the company in 2013. I achieved 70 per cent more than expected for the existing shareholders (30 per cent more than my own minimum) whilst at the same time giving the new shareholders a deal that they were very happy with.

"The negotiations took place over two days and initially concentrated on discussions on due diligence issues, the SPA and the shareholders' agreement. The buyers then sought a significant discount from their original pre due diligence "indicative" offer that I refused to entertain and threatened to walk away.

"I realised that everything was going to plan when they quickly retreated from that position and at the end of the day we gave them a small discount and got a great deal for all involved."

⚬⚬⚬

Following the negotiation, good or bad, a response has to be made capturing what occurred – a formal response to the other side, and possibly a public or media response. Where there has been collaboration prior to the negotiation, and ground rules outlined, this will have been covered, and hopefully there will not have been a walk out and a rush to get the story on the media first.

The formal response to the other side needs to capture what are the assumptions now. Are there conditions attached? Where do we go from here? Who is going to do what and by when?

A good chair will have captured these as the negotiation has been progressing, and it will be a simple enough matter to agree and issue a joint statement.

Chapter Eight

Coaching Yourself and Others

In this chapter, we take a look at coaching, and holding coaching conversations, as a means to improve communication in the workplace and to allow yourself and others to thrive.

Influencer and former baseball player Sahil Bloom posted a thread recently about how we spend our time over the life course and it was elucidating, to say the least! Between the ages of 20 and 60, we spend an outsize amount of time with our co-workers. So if we have the luxury of choice, we should choose work - and co-workers - that we find meaningful and important.

He says, "Aim to have co-workers who create energy in your life", and it is a great thought.

I'd say that whether we fully realise it or not, we all want to work in a company led by a coach, and in a department led by a coach.

You know the kind of department I am talking about – the one where people are always peering over the partitions as they walk by, because there is such a buzz going on. Laughter emanates, people are happy, they produce great results. You can be sure there is a leader in there somewhere, who understands that a coaching style gets the best from people.

But what is a coach, and how do you become one? How do you start developing the right attributes and qualities?

Entrepreneur Safa Sharif, Director of the Masy Holdings construction company in Bahrain, is honest enough to voice his reservations about coaching.

"I don't enjoy it, as I feel impatient, and it drains me, but I do it all the time because I know it is such an important tool to let me know people better, and to enhance the relationship. I dig deep and ask a lot of 'why' questions, always trying to narrow the problem or get closer to the roots of it, and then I end by highlighting the positives."

Safa has identified the main obstacle to coaching as a workplace convention – it takes time, patience, energy and commitment. It is so much easier to snap an instruction, or to think 'I'd be quicker doing it myself.'

I have run half-day or day-long training programmes for people at all levels who want to learn a bit about coaching techniques. Not everyone has the time to undertake a full coaching diploma, but everyone can learn how to hold a coaching conversation; to take a more collaborative approach to problem solving, finding solutions and giving direction in the workplace.

The kind of things we cover are understanding the business case for coaching, why this style of leadership is a fit for our times. We look at the potential impact of a coaching style on self-direction, satisfaction, engagement and retention. And we talk about spotting coachable moments and opportunities, and having the tools to maximise them. It is all to play for, when you think about it, with the benefits to be found in happy co-workers who know how to get on with each other and get things done.

Getting Started

One of the founding fathers of modern coaching, Sir John Whitmore, came up with the GROW model in the late 1980s, and it is one of the most widely used coaching techniques today for problem solving, goal setting and performance improvement. It can be used by anyone, anytime, anywhere, and generally gets fast, obvious results.

So if there is a problem brewing, or the project is stuck, or the new colleague is swamped, our instinct is often to start telling everyone what to do. The problem is that most of us don't like being told what to do, and will probably just back up and do nothing. We prefer to work things out for ourselves, and in that way take ownership of the decision and the subsequent outcomes.

You know when the intern comes to you and says "I have this problem, it's all going wrong, it's such a mess, what should I do?" And you say, "That's not a problem at all, just do this and this and it will all be ok."

A quick fix, but is it actually ok? Maybe not. Maybe the intern now feels a bit foolish because he thought it was a problem, but it seems it wasn't really a problem at all.

What if you responded "What do you think you should do?" And gave him the opportunity to think of a solution? What if you took the time to spend a few minutes working through with him the options available, so that he made the best decision on the action to take? He is now learning to think for himself, and to self-direct, rather than just to ask for an instruction every time there is a problem, taking up a lot more time in the long run.

Coaching is all about asking questions; the kind of questions that will allow someone to come at the issue in a new way, and to achieve the satisfaction of finding their own solution, and the impetus to get on with things that comes with that clarity.

To use the *GROW* model:

G stands for Goal. What is the problem we are going to work on right now and what result do we want to get?

R is for the Reality of the current situation. So your next questions might be - How did this problem arise? What were the circumstances? What have you done so far? What is getting in your way?

O is for Options. You move on to questions like – What could you try? What else could you do? What options do you have? What are the advantages to this option or the disadvantages to that option?

W is for Will. You begin to wrap up the exchange with questions like - What will you do? Which option is looking like the best one? On a scale of 1 – 10, how committed are you to that option? If it is not a 10, what would make it a 10?

Self Coaching

The GROW model works equally well as a self-coaching tool when you are working on an issue of your own. Find somewhere quiet and work through the steps until you achieve clarity about what can be done, and make a commitment as to what you will do.

And don't panic if the decision has to be not to do something just yet, because you don't have the right information to hand. The decision can be to get that information, and to then to action the commitment by a certain time or date.

Some other tools and techniques you can use to help yourself or others become unstuck are:

Imagery – Imagine what the goal or solution would look like, what you would like it to be? You know the one about if you can dream it you can be it? A few seconds day dreaming about what the ideal end point looks like is positive and healthy.

Past event – Think about when something similar happened in the past, a time when you overcame a challenge. What did you do then that you can do now?

Pride – When did you feel proud? What happened? What skills did you use then, which will help now?

Who else – Is there anyone you know, or admire, who has done something similar? What did they do? How did they do it? What can you learn from their approach?

Worst thing – What is the worst thing that can happen? Be careful using this one, it can be negative. But can also bring great relief. Maybe the situation is not that bad after all.

Different view – Walk in someone else's shoes. Think of someone you know, or who you see in the organisation who seems to be getting it right. What might they do?

Clean space – Go to a space that knows more. Switch your current location, get away from the desk, take a walk in the park, or even a walk around the building. Use movement to stir the blood and ignite the brain, so that better thoughts can come through.

I personally love that last one, a clean space, or a space that knows more, and use it as often as I can. Luckily I work from home in the beautiful countryside of County Meath in Ireland, so there is no shortage of beautiful spaces that 'know more' quite close to me. The ancient trees alone share their wisdom every time you rustle by.

Find your clean space and make a habit of going there when those brain cogs are turning, trying to find the solution to a personal or career problem, or when you are trying to help a friend or associate with theirs.

There is another framework you can try, if GROW is not doing its business on any particular day. This is known as the **ABCDE** model, which is particularly useful helping in dealing with limiting beliefs, yours or theirs.

A *is for an Activating Event.* I want to ask for a pay rise, but just haven't found the way to do so. I am waking up every morning thinking about it, and beginning to feel really put upon, and not appreciated by the business because I have been working so hard, and feel I deserve more, but no one else seems to have noticed.

B *is for current Belief.* I have been telling myself I am definitely not going to get the increase, the boss doesn't like me, she is very distracted lately with her own stuff and won't want to listen to me.

C *is for Consequence.* As a result of the way I have been letting my brain run on, I am suffering from low self-esteem, I am feeling under-valued and very frustrated, which is seeping into my personal life.

D *is for Dispute.* I need to challenge this thinking. Maybe it is all just my perception? Why do I think that the boss doesn't like me? Who else, if anybody, has said anything? Have I imagined all of this or is there any evidence anywhere?

E *is for Exchange.* I need to exchange my old ideas for a completely new rationale. I need to try to see the situation differently, assume a different set of beliefs about it, and use those new beliefs to bolster my confidence and go and ask for the pay rise.

I saw this happen with a young man who works for a start up in the supply sector. He has been with them for two years now, has learned so much about the business, and has used his exceptional inter-personal skills to great effect with customers and colleagues alike.

He felt he was due a raise, and had mentioned it briefly to a fairly positive reaction, but then everyone got very busy, a key person was out sick, another Director was off on a buying trip, and it all got kicked to touch. He was feeling very frustrated, and the longer it went on, the harder it was for him to bring it up again.

He had to self-coach in the way we have discussed to get rid of all the negative thoughts and to bring himself to the point where he asked for a formal meeting to discuss his position. Chatting to him after the meeting, it was clear that he was positively glowing! They had told him how fabulous he was, they had given him the raise, and had also agreed to pay for his study course. His previous negative perceptions had been entirely in his own head!

Types of Questions

I have said that coaching yourself or others is all about using lots of questions. In an organisation where there is a coaching culture, people use questions to preserve an open environment, and to strengthen communication and relationships. The type of question you choose will depend on the information or the result you want. It helps to refresh ourselves on some different question types, and what result they might produce:

An Open question facilitates a good thoughtful answer, because you can't just say yes or no to it. They encourage someone to respond with a bit of detail. Journalists try to use open questions when interviewing someone, so that they maximise their chances of getting quality information. Examples of open questions include: Tell me how you are getting on with the project? What have you liked about working here so far? What have you been doing lately John?

A *Closed question* is the opposite, and probably should be avoided in both coaching and journalism! But they are helpful when you need direct information. They generally can only produce binary answers, yes or no, true or false. For example: Were you at the meeting last Thursday? Is Penny out sick? Do you want me to write that report?

A *Probing question* takes things deeper, encouraging perspective, nuance and reasoning. Probing questions are often follow-up questions to previous answers. Good examples are: You said you didn't get a good response from your manager, what exactly were you hoping for? The client is unhappy you believe, what makes you think that? Is there anything you can add to what you have already told me?

A *Leading question* is nudging the person towards a particular answer or response. They need to be used sparingly, as they could be perceived to be manipulative. Examples include: Don't you think this is a great place to work? I think that meeting with the client went really well, how about you? Wouldn't it be good if we were to agree on the approach beforehand?

A *Reflective question* has no right or wrong answer. The idea is to get someone to explore, to think and to consider options. They often come up in job interviews. Examples include: What do you think would happen if you were to suggest to your manager that the product should be dropped? Which area of the business do you think needs most focus at this point? If we got a bad comment on our social media page, what kind of responses should we consider?

A *Hypothetical question* is often used to encourage lateral thinking and problem solving. You are presented with a scenario and asked how you might react to it, or what you might do to solve it. Consider these examples: If you came upon a row that had just blown up in the warehouse between two colleagues, what would you do? If a customer got very angry with you on the phone, how would you handle it? Say you were to consider doing some extra study at night, what might you hope to gain?

A *Sequential question* is one of a series of questions to uncover the layers within the situation or topic being explored. They follow one after the other, going down a particular road or direction. For example: What did you feel worked well in the meeting? What part did the client respond best to, do you think? Was there any part of it that didn't work so well? Would you do anything differently next time?

A *Behavioural question* is a question about how you acted in a given situation. In an interview context they are used to assess how you might conduct yourself under pressure. In a coaching context they are used to help with self-awareness. Good examples are: Tell me about a time when something went very wrong for you, what did you learn from it? Give me an example of when you had to step up and take over for the day because perhaps your supervisor was away unexpectedly? What is the most difficult situation you've ever had to resolve in the workplace?

Knowing about these question types, and what results you can expect when you use them, can seriously increase your ability to communicate effectively with your colleagues and friends. They are the very bones of a coaching culture in an organisation – the idea that people might use curiosity and interest when confronted with a tricky situation, rather than hostility, anger or defensiveness.

The Qualities of a Coach

There are many different types of coach as we know, professional an amateur, and we have come across them in so many areas of our lives. There is the business coach, the executive coach, the communications coach, the life coach, the sports coach, the drama coach and so many more. They each have a place in our world, and each work every day to bring out the best in others.

I became a business and executive coach in a roundabout way. After an early career in broadcast journalism, I took time out to raise my family. Later I began putting my insider knowledge of being behind the camera and the microphone to good effect, training and coaching people to go on the media with their personal or business story.

I broadened that out to a full range of workplace communications trainings, and probably had a few thousand coaching hours under my belt before I decided to formalise my offering by undergoing a fairly strenuous accreditation process with the European Mentoring and Coaching Council.

I am so glad that I did, as I came to realise that the optimal behaviours we have come to expect in every workplace, and indeed deserve, are platformed upon an agreed set of standards and agreed codes of practice. Internal or external coaches need to know about these standards, to adhere to them and to be qualified to deliver out on them.

Yes we can all use coaching style conversations in our everyday work to improve communication and maximise results. But if you are considering choosing a coach to work closely with, in any sphere, then it may help to understand the standards we aim for.

Do a search on coaching standards and *The Five Cs* will come up. The problem is The Five Cs are different in every article you read! It seems that we all like the model of the Five Cs, but can't agree on what they stand for. So all I can do here is share with you my personal favourites.

Character A coach has to have intellectual, ethical and moral rigour. You have to be what you want others to be. You won't get away with the lines we all hear ourselves using on our kids, "Do as I say, not as I do". Or even worse, "Because I said so!" You have to live every day a value system that is true, recognisable and understandable. People have to be able to trust you and your consistency. Think of the best teacher, mentor or boss you ever had. You could trust their judgement, their reactions, the direction they gave you, and they were consistent in their approach.

Caring A coach is aware of the full human dimension of each member of the team. People don't show up as marketing executives, or teachers, or shop assistants in isolation. They are parents, sisters, sons, partners, dog owners, runners, bakers, gardeners, singers and all kinds of other fascinating, interesting and demanding things. The coach becomes aware of these things, and knows that they always frame what is going on.

Commitment A coach is mindful and present when with the team or the individual. They put the mobile on silent, turn off the screen and give complete attention to the person who needs it. That means eye contact and highly developed listening skills. They have a complete passion for their area of expertise.

Confidence A coach often has a big over-arching vision that others buy into; an intuition about what is going to work for the person or the team and how they can help you get there. They pump up your belief, get you on board, show you your part in the whole, and help you to be better than you ever thought you could be.

Communication A coach has highly developed communication skills and uses them to tease out the issues, and support the coachee in finding solutions. They can articulate the vision so that everyone really understands it, and break it down into achievable and measurable chunks, so the steps ahead are clear.

I could also talk about compassion and curiosity and clarity and collaboration but I think you get the picture.

Growing a Coaching Culture

Back to you now as someone who is interested in what coaching conversations can achieve in the workplace, and how you can encourage a coaching culture to thrive. If you have any influence over the choice of potential new colleagues, or are involved in recruitment, what are the markers you should look for?

They say you should hire for attitude and teach everything else. So with that in mind, the top attitudinal markers for me are:

The ability to make choices A love of technology can allow someone to exercise nothing but their thumbs, shooting aliens in their bedroom on gaming consoles; or to explore, access and appreciate the wonder and the power of information, available today in a way that was never there before. Does this person make good choices?

Analysis and judgment The societal parameters laid down by institutions like churches, states, and banks have been tarnished. Personal integrity is all we have left. What is this person's value system like, and does it match what you are trying to do in this business?

Problem solving It takes confidence and skill to believe that whatever befalls us, whatever is in store for us, we have the intellectual rigour and the resilience to find a way around it. What personal problems has this person faced and solved?

Willingness to fail Does this person know how many failures it takes to get a win? Will they fall apart if they do fail, or learn and move on?

Leadership Not based on title, years on the job, or pay grade but based on belief, insight and passion for the project. What projects has this person led to completion?

Creativity The ability to take away the barriers of judgment, bias and insecurity, and to let all the ideas in to the silo. Is this person open to new ideas?

The confidence to dream And to persuade others to believe in the vision and get on board. Does this person talk about possibilities?

The ability to communicate None of the above is of any real use if it can't be communicated. Has this person worked at finding a personal way of communication that is effective?

A top education is no guarantor of any of the above. Some of the qualities are innate, some are cultivated in strong family or community units, some are picked up as you go along, particularly if you have the benefit of good role models or mentors.

A report from the Harvard Business School on the future of the MBA has identified that completing students often lack an awareness of their impact on others, and show a requirement for work in the area of personal skills and the practice of leadership.

It is all about connecting with our fellow human beings and understanding and being understood in real time, not in virtual time. The connector is human emotion. And we have to find the confidence to use this emotion in our personal communication in business, in order that we will reach people, connect with them and get them to come on our journey with us.

Yes, it is argued that there is no room for emotion in business – feelings should be left at the far side of the door – and certainly we can all do without high drama or head throws in the workplace. But there is room, and indeed a serious need, for emotional connection.

The thing that strikes you most about successful entrepreneurs is their belief in, and absolute passion for, their product or service. Money or acclaim are secondary drivers. The prime driver inevitably is the belief that the world really, really, needs the product or service.

Entrepreneur Noelle O'Connor is the founder of the tanning product TanOrganic. Listening to her speak at an event one time, I heard her describe how women went to great lengths to eat healthily, when everything you ingest that way is filtered by the liver before it gets to the blood stream.

Yet they put tanning lotions all over the skin, which is the largest body organ and the one without a filter, sending the ingredients straight to the blood stream, without first checking what is in the bottle.

She couldn't sleep knowing that we could be destroying our health, and set about developing a tanning product that is completely safe. She came up with the world's first fully certified organic tan.

And that is what we need in the workplace. We need to develop people who have an emotional connection with what they are doing – because that is the true genesis of confidence, creativity, and communication.

The Art of Feedback

A true marker of an organisation with a coaching culture is one where giving and receiving feedback is the norm, not something that only happens once a year at performance reviews, or when there is a problem.

A coachee of mine who joined a new organisation a while back admits that she didn't ask enough questions at her interviews, and finds herself now in an environment where feedback is spectacularly absent. She is working hard at introducing it in her own team, and bringing it up at wider meetings whenever she can.

Giving feedback means telling a co-worker about the effect their work style, performance or behaviour is having on the team and its output and dynamic.

Feedback can be shared up, down or across an organisation. It can build good relationships and get everyone working together to achieve team goals. It can also help individuals re-boot their performance and increase their personal effectiveness and job satisfaction.

Frank Lampard, former top Chelsea FC top goal scorer tells a great story about the time manager Jose Mourinho stopped him in the shower room after a Saturday game and says, "There's something I want to talk to you about".

Jose was fully dressed, and Frank was in the altogether, so it was a little awkward, and Frank may not have been ready to listen.

But Jose went on to say that Frank was one of the best players in the world, and there wasn't a game that he saw that didn't reconfirm that belief in his mind.

Frank says that he went home floating on air, and was still floating when he arrived back in for training on the Monday morning. The power of positive feedback, despite the location!

Unfortunately a lot of people don't like giving, or getting, feedback. The giver fears hurt and rejection and the receiver feels like they are being criticised or judged.

Approached correctly, it can make a huge difference to how a team works. When feedback follows a defined and agreed pattern, that everyone knows and uses, it can deliver great results and improve relationships enormously.

The steps below are very simple to follow and make the experience better for everyone.

The giver of feedback should:

- Check intent: Why am I choosing to give this feedback? Am I doing this to genuinely help this person, or is it about me asserting my authority?

- Check time: Is this the right time to give the feedback? Is the recipient open now to taking this on board? (And place. Not the shower room!)

- Ask permission: Is the recipient ok with the idea of feedback on this project in the first place?

- Be specific: No broad strokes. Give clear feedback on line items, not the overall project or event

- Note the impact: On both the giver and the receiver! How did you feel? How did he or she feel?

- Specify how to move forward: Clarity is everything. Agree what should be done differently in future.

- Check for understanding: On both sides. Is the recipient clear now on what needs to change? Are you clear on all the circumstances that led to this situation?

The receiver of feedback should:

- Release tension by asking questions. Get absolute clarity as to where the concerns are.

- Summarise the feedback. "So, you are concerned that my delay in telling you about the problems we are having with the project is causing confusion…

- Ask what the request is. How should things be done differently?

- Respond to the feedback. Accept the request, or make an alternative suggestion.

- Express understanding. Offer thanks for the feedback!

Despite the best of intentions, feedback can go pear-shaped. People go home for the weekend, fuming and worrying and taking it out on their families, and arrive back in on Monday ashen-faced and stressed. This is not what should happen and maybe Friday afternoon is not the time for the feedback session.

Following the protocols above should prevent it going wrong. Ideally, both the giver and the receiver of the feedback should feel more aligned after the session and more in agreement about where things should go in the future.

If feedback does go wrong, it is usually because the timing didn't suit the recipient - they may have been late leaving to collect their child from the crèche and were never going to listen to you. Or perhaps they were still emoting or upset over whatever had gone wrong.

Sometimes it is because there was no privacy during the chat, people nearby could hear what was going on. Or it could have been because the language used was a bit judgmental, or perhaps permission to give the feedback was not asked for.

Problems can also occur when there is no organisational culture of giving or receiving feedback, or where the person offering the feedback is a bit vague or general and does not look for clear next steps.

So remember to give and get feedback with good heart. If we have the growth mindset we discussed earlier we will view feedback as a gift - to be given with compassion, and received with grace.

My friend above, who is starting to introduce the idea of feedback in her new organisation, is using vulnerability as a tool. She says things like, "I see that you are surprised by the idea of feedback, and to be honest I wish I was more practiced at giving it…"

This approach relaxes both herself and the team member she is working with, and sets them up for success from the start.

～

The workplace as we previously knew it is changing very rapidly. Brian Murphy of Microsoft, who worked in global banking in the 2008 financial crisis, and in the global pharmaceutical industry during Covid, says this one feels different because it is the very nature of work that is changing.

Flexibility in how you work and what you work on will be yours, inside or outside an organisation, he believes, if you work on developing skills, accessing mentoring or coaching, and identifying particular concerns or projects to get involved with.

"For the first time in my career, employees have true agency to decide what work they want to do, where to do it, and when" he says. "For organisations, the traditional approach to meeting capability needs, short-term cycles of hiring and restructuring, simply isn't sustainable anymore."

He talks about how the Job, and its particular description, used to be the key unit for progress within an organisation, but that now all the research points to Skills overtaking that; Skills are become the currency for employee career development and growth. And the more you have of them, the more control you will have over your own progress.

The quid pro quo for organisations, he believes, is in the potential to gain optimal agility. All they have to do is hire well, bring in great talent, and then trust people to make a call on when they need to be in the office or when they might work best at home.

Chapter Nine

The Media Interview

In this chapter you will get the lowdown on how to prepare for and deliver a really good media interview on behalf of your business, department or club, and you'll learn about the pitfalls to avoid. Many people hate or are even afraid of doing interviews, so if you are prepared to take it on, you can get great kudos and raise your profile. Journalists aren't out to get you - they are out to get the story!

"**AND** we're live".

Those are the words from the floor manager as the red light comes on, the presenter looks to camera, and the moment you have been waiting for – with either dread or anticipation – is here. You are about to speak to the nation, and it is going to work out really well, or then again maybe it isn't.

You are a guest on the TV programme this evening to defend your company or personal reputation, or perhaps as an 'expert' to give your views on entrepreneurship or the economy; or maybe as a spokesperson for a cause or concern. Either way, tomorrow morning you will do one of two things.

You will sail out your front door, delighted with yourself. You'll head to work with a smile on your face, and stroll out of the lift and through the department, basking in the glow of congratulation and pats on the back.

Or you will sprint to the car, dodging the knowing look from Johnny across the street, and use the fire escape to creep into your office, to barricade yourself behind a pile of reports and deadlines and avoid the canteen at lunchtime.

A media outing is a huge opportunity. Well prepared, and with a good insight to how the game is played, you can and will do very well. But it is also a minefield, and careers can be ended with very public mistakes by those who wing it, or who take on more than they can handle.

If you are going to be the spokesperson for your company or organisation, and you will be appearing on a prime time show, do yourself a big favour and get some training from any one of the professionals out there who do a great job!

You wouldn't buy a business without getting advice from a lawyer or an accountant, or run a marathon without working with a fitness coach. So don't chance doing a major outing without good support. But in the meantime, there are plenty of things you can learn here, which will give you insight to how the media works in practice, and which are useful skills for local interviews and less pressurised occasions.

When we work with people preparing for the media, we start by recording a practice interview. Straight away people can see what they are doing wrong.

In a group training:

- Aisling said she didn't convey what she wanted to at all. She got steered into talking about a former role rather than her current business, which she was there to promote.

- Dorothea was concerned about using lots of words to say nothing, and over-using words such as 'like' and 'basically', since English is not her first language.

- Patrick felt that he had been ambushed by the interviewer, whom he wanted to punch throughout the encounter! He thought that he'd wasted the whole time looking for retribution.

- Lynn thought she'd been waffling. Expecting lots of tough questions, she carried on talking about nothing waiting for a question. When it came, it was from a completely different place, and she waffled again.

- Marie felt she didn't explain herself at all. She is used to talking to people who already know about the subject, and found it hard to explain the basics to a new audience.

- Avril felt she had been led down a road, fell into traps, and became very defensive. She got flustered and then couldn't collect her thoughts as well as she normally does.

- Michael thought he had come across as a know it all. He said nervousness had made him a bit aggressive.

Actually, none of these first interviews were half as bad as the people themselves thought. Some of them were really quite good, with the interviewees sounding authoritative and knowledgeable, despite making the mistakes they ably spotted themselves.

Media starts to become easy once you understand the rules of engagement, and once you get in some practice. A lot of it is common sense, and the kind of stuff you know already. And once you start thinking about this, you will start listening to media interviews in a new way, and training your ear to spot what works and what doesn't.

Try this one out.

The next time you are listening to your favourite radio station driving in your car, or sitting in your kitchen, pick an interview and listen to it closely from start to finish. It will probably be six or seven minutes long.

Now turn down the sound, really think about the interview, and ask yourself a few questions. What was the one single message that jumped out at you from this interview? How was that message illustrated? Was the interview interesting? Did you believe the spokesperson?

Your answers to those questions tell you straight away whether this was a good interviewee or not. If you have no idea what they were talking about, they wasted their time going into the studio that day.

If they spoke in an abstract way, and didn't give you a memorable picture to take away with you, they were wasting their time. If they bored you, they definitely should have stayed in bed that morning. And if you didn't believe them, well, what can we say?

When it is your turn to do an interview, you want to aim for:

Clarity

Credibility

Colour

Listening at home, or in my car, I want to be very clear about what you are saying to me. I want to hear in your voice and your conviction that you are genuine and therefore I will warm to you and believe in you. And I want to hear your thoughts presented in a colourful way that will resonate with me, and make me remember exactly what it was you said.

And this gives you the water cooler moment, the thing that people will be talking about later in the day.

Siobhan Talbot, the CEO of dairy giant Glanbia, did an interview with one of the main early morning radio chat shows for International Women's Day and later I overheard this conversation:

"Did you hear your woman on this morning, wasn't she amazing? She is running one of the biggest businesses in the country, and she makes it sound so easy. And she had cancer a couple of years ago."

"Yeah, and she has kids and everything, and she sounds so nice. She comes across as really warm and friendly."

"She should be running the country. Maybe she would think of going for politics."

I think they liked her!

Doing a good interview is about getting your ducks in a row beforehand, knowing how to prepare without over preparing, and knowing the rules of engagement.

It is about realising that you are not at the complete mercy of the interviewer, as comfortable in the studio as he is in his own living room. There are plenty of things you can do to get some control, and to steer the interview to where you want it to go.

Here are a few ideas for you to think about:

An interview is not an exam

Yes you are the Principal of the college, or the Head of Marketing, or the CEO of the firm, but even with the title and all the responsibility that goes with it, you are not expected to know everything. If you crowd your head with all the facts and figures beforehand, terrified that you will be caught out, you will not be 'in the moment' in studio, or mindful enough to make the most of the opportunity.

The interviewer is not an examiner and she is not testing you. All she is doing is trying to make you interesting to keep her listeners tuned in, or keep her readers going to the end of the article.

Journalists are not out to get you. They are out to get the story.

So if you are honest, interesting and engaging, they won't have to get out the spade and start digging, nor will they become argumentative or difficult. You will have made their job easier by giving up good solid material that is interesting for the listener, viewer or reader.

The alternative is to be flat, boring and evasive, and then to have the interest extracted out of you by a clever, probing journalist, in the same way a dentist uses those noisy instruments. The choice is yours!

Equally dispiriting is when the journalist drops

you suddenly. You were promised the interview would be ten minutes long, and after two or three minutes they are moving on to the next item on the running order. It may be that there is a big story breaking behind the scenes but it could be that you are just not interesting enough. Be warned!

Answering the First Question

Your opening answer is probably the most important part of the whole interview. It is a big opportunity for you to lay out your wares, and to drop in some key words and ideas that the interviewer may come back to as the interview progresses.

Interviewers expect this, and can get caught out if you are too abrupt.

Once when I was doing some stand-in presenting on my local radio station a spokesperson for a hospital support group was the interviewee. I started by asking him how the campaign was going, and he said fine.

And then he stopped. And waited.

I nearly fell off my chair!

I had just been reading my running order to see how long this interview should last, and listening at the same time on talk-back to my producer telling me that we'd be taking an unscheduled ad break, and would I like my coffee sent in?

This is actually quite normal. There is often a bit of housekeeping going on at the start of an interview, particularly on radio, and it gives a well prepared interviewee a bit of a 'free run'. This is a chance to set the tone for the whole exchange, particularly if you get a 'soft' first question like the one I proffered.

My friend above lost a great opportunity, when he just answered 'fine', to open his interview strongly and really catch the attention.

But on the other hand you shouldn't ever count on a straightforward 'how is the project going' type of opening question.

A first question is a ball that can be lobbed in from absolutely anywhere in the field, and you have to be ready for it. Some people never get over the shock of the randomness of the first question, and are then on the back foot for the rest of the interview.

So listen well, answer the question you are asked, and go on to lay out the parameters of what you are there to talk about, taking your time to do it, and making sure there is an interesting hook or two in the mix.

Inexperienced interviewees will give an opening answer that lasts for maybe 19 or 20 seconds – or two seconds flat if they are like my hospital friend. Listen out over the next few days and you will begin to spot them.

The old hands will speak for well over a minute, benefitting from a kind of unwritten convention that this is a polite amount of time for a first answer.

And sometimes also benefitting from the distraction of the programme host!

Getting into the Driving Seat

So who has their hands on the wheel during an interview? It can be you, if you know how to go about it.

Larger than life Irish Government Minister, Padraig Flynn, known as Pee Flynn, was notorious for answering journalists questions with the words "I'm glad you asked me that", and then proceeding to go off on a tangent of his own that completely ignored the question.

The problem with ignoring the question is that the journalist wants to know why, and will go after the answer relentlessly.

You will no doubt have heard of the famous Jeremy Paxman interview on Newsnight when he asked the UK Home Secretary Michael Howard the same question 14 times in a row.

He kept Howard wriggling and squirming for ages, in what has become one of those clips played over and over again on YouTube.

So, to avoid this, it is a good idea, a really good idea, to answer the question you are asked.

Taking over the driving seat in an interview is not about avoiding questions, it is about answering them. And answering them so well and in such an interesting way, that you can roll seamlessly on to wherever you want to go next.

The interviewer, happy with the original answer, and the quality of your information, may well be inclined to go along with you. It is that simple. But:

- If you don't know the answer – say so.

- If you know the answer, but haven't the authority to divulge the information – say so.

- If you don't want to answer – say so. (There is no law that says you have to!)

It is ignoring the question, or studiously avoiding it, that causes the problem, and leads to the kind of antics that are mind-numbingly irritating for those of us listening at home, and often serve to prompt scorn.

Controlling Tempo, Tone, and Tension

As the interview progresses, you retain control by answering the questions you are asked, and continuing on to a point you want to make. You plan these points before you go into the studio. And to use a sporting analogy, you have to think of each exchange as playing soccer and not table tennis.

In table tennis, the ball is going pit pat, pit pat, back and forward across the table. In soccer, you get that ball, retain possession, withstand tackles, dribble it all the way up the pitch, aim for the goal, and score. That is what each of your answers should look and feel like.

How the answers sound is very dependent on how well you control tempo, tone and tension, and I have to put my hand up here and say I am a fine one to talk. As a guest in studio, as opposed to a presenter, this is something I often get wrong.

My enthusiasm for the subject, and my urgency to get it across in the short time available, means that I sometimes speak too fast, and allow my voice to rise. But if I explain it to you here, hopefully you will do a better job when your turn comes.

Tempo: When the pace is steady and controlled, you keep your thoughts in order and get your ideas out coherently, and in complete sentences rather than in broken phrases. When the distance between the question and answer keeps shortening, hearts beat faster, palms become sweaty, anxiety creeps in, and voices go shrill.

Controlling the tempo is about playing soccer, as described above, and not being afraid to use short pauses and reflection in answering.

Tone: Finding the right voice will influence the tempo. As a guest on a programme, your job is to sound conversational, explanatory, knowledgeable, expert. And to find the kind of language that gives you the space to expand.

Phrases that work well are: "Let me explain what I mean by that" or "To put that another way..." or "There are a couple of important points about that which I think are worth sharing..."

Tension: It is much harder for hostility or aggression to enter the frame when the tone and tempo are being controlled. It takes two to tango, and an interviewer can't possibly have a row with himself.

He can always try the adversarial approach to the interview, and is quite within his rights to do so, but if you do not mirror his tone or tempo, and stay in your own zone, you'll be fine.

You have to do your swan impersonation! Stay cool and calm on top and do all the paddling underneath.

Putting interest into the interview

The media is a crowded space with more competition than ever, and we are spoiled for choice by the number of radio and TV stations we have access to. This makes us very fickle.

Just one irritating guest or poor song choice, and we change station or channel hop until we are happy.

Those of us who still read newspapers have the same pull on our attention span. If the article we are reading is not holding our attention, we throw the paper on the sofa, and pick up our devices to start scrolling instead.

So we have to make interviews interesting and we do it with:

Pictures

Passion

Persuasion

Pictures I remember seeing an interview once on a heritage programme where this very elderly farmer sitting in his kitchen in a remote location on the side of a mountain was being asked about using modern technology. He said he preferred the radio to the television because the pictures were better!

He was clearly listening to good radio, where his imagination was being stimulated to colour the scene.

When you are being interviewed for radio, TV, print or online, the more pictures, stories and examples you can provide, the better the outcome will be. That's because they go straight to the reader or the listener and make them feel part of your world.

You connect with the audience by putting a picture in their head of what you are talking about and making them care about it, describing in the here and now what is going on, rather than speaking in an abstract way.

This is perhaps why the 'sick child' slot, as people in the industry refer to it, has become so popular on chat shows. Regardless of how jaded or cynical we are, when we listen to a couple describe very personally, and usually very emotionally, what is happening with their child's situation, we become completely involved.

Although we are listening to their story, we are relating it back to our own lives and thinking about relatives or friends going through the same thing. Through personal and intimate story-telling, they are building a bridge which we cross over.

And yes, in communication terms, the task is a lot harder when it is a business situation you are describing. How do you create a picture, and add in feeling to make it connect?

You do it by getting to "the other day I met a man..." as quickly as possible, a real example of how the product or service or idea works in action. Because the story you tell will make the point far more efficiently and memorably than anything you can do in the abstract.

The seventeen second rule first came to light when former actor Ronald Regan was US President. An acknowledged expert communicator, he used to say that if he had not got to Bill and Joan within seventeen seconds, the interview was not going well. He meant that he had to bring the message straight to the ordinary man and woman on the street, or he knew people would tune out. Practically every politician the world over follows his lead and now uses this technique.

Interviewers know that this is what you are doing, but they can't help themselves. They are seduced by the power of the story too. And they find it hard to interrupt, knowing that this is what the listener or the reader wants.

European Commissioner Mairéad McGuinness was being interviewed on radio one morning when, as a former journalist herself, and indeed a gifted communicator, she answered the point and went straight into a story. "Out campaigning last Wednesday I met a person who said…"

The interviewer, clearly anxious to show that there are no flies on him, came right back with "Oh, come on Mairéad, so you are going to start into *I met a man*, this better be good."

But then he sat right back in the chair and let her off! She got a clear run at the next few minutes of airtime.

It was as if the interviewer, having clearly signalled that he knew what she was up to, was satisfied at that, and had no further need to interrupt. So he let her finish that story, and roll right on to make two or three more really good points. Game set and match to Mairéad.

Passion We can't fake interest or knowledge in a subject. We either care about something or we don't. And the only subjects we should ever talk about publicly are those we do actually care about.

Because it is this concern that gives us direction and fluency, and a degree of protection. If you are speaking passionately about something you really believe in, no matter where an interviewer or fellow panellist stands on the issue, a part of them has to respect your beliefs.

I have a friend who has become a panellist and commentator, having retrained in journalism after a very different career. She is really good at it, and makes it her business to stay on top of any subject on which she might be asked to give a view.

But she told me recently about her sense of panic when she knows a topic is coming up which she hasn't covered before. She rings her sister and asks her, "What do I think about the proposed tax hike?"

It is not that she is actually asking the sister to spoon-feed her some views. She is using the sounding board of a trusted family member to vocalise her views before she goes on air; to bounce them around, hear how they sound – out loud – and get her thoughts aligned before that red light goes on.

It's good practice, because when she is in studio she now has ownership of the ideas and they come across confidently and well.

We like listening to enthusiasm, and we like listening to expertise. We like listening to an enthusiastic expert most of all.

Entrepreneurs are often criticised for the casual way they use the word 'passion'. They are passionate about start-ups, and widgets, and the App that is going to change the world, and the international cleaning business, or whatever it is that they are working on at the moment.

But they are not lying. They usually are seriously into those things. They have to be, to withstand the pressures of staying with a single product or concept all the way. So they become very focused. The good ones have a way of making that one thing very interesting, and talking about it in a way that engages us and makes us want to know more.

Persuasion We are quite selfish in the way we listen, view and read. We scan things for their relevance to our own lives and worlds. A good interviewee knows this and is always thinking about the audience and putting them first.

I call it finding your Touchstone Tom. Who is your ideal listener or reader? The person you really want to convince today during this interview that this is a good product, or service or idea. Is it a potential investor, a customer, a politician, a stake-holder?

Whoever it is, and make it a real person, not an imaginary one, he is who you should be talking to throughout the interview, in the kind of direct language that will capture him and convince him.

If you met him at a function, or in the street, how would you explain the concept to him and win him around? That is what you have to do on air, avoiding the trap of over engaging with the interviewer, as if he or she is the end goal, and not the conduit to the audience.

Preparing your messages for any interview should start with the audience, the demographic for that particular program or publication. That is the 'what' piece, the one or two key things you are going to get across today.

And then you have to plan the 'how' – the stories and examples you will use, as described earlier, to get those messages across, and persuade the listener to agree with you.

Removing the Bus Driver's Hat

What is it about walking into a radio or TV studio, or sitting down in front of a journalist with a recording device on the table, that makes a lot of people take out the bus driver's hat and plonk it firmly on their head, in a similar way to the corporate presenter, mentioned earlier?

By that I mean that as they are now the official public representative of the company or the concern, they think they should speak in a formal, stilted way. They become very grand, very complex, use convoluted explanations, and the whole purpose of the communication goes out the window.

People who do this are actually afraid. They are hiding behind the hat, and the uniform, thinking that this is safe. It will impress the folks back in the office, and will sound very professional and highbrow.

It actually does the opposite. It makes everything too abstract to hold our interest, so we zone out, or change the channel.

Have you ever been driving in traffic with the radio on, listening to a business programme and there is some chap banging on about his metrics, and his quarter four projections, and his knowledge process outsourcing, and so on. And you find yourself wondering what's on the telly tonight, or if your partner remembered to bring the dog to the vet?

He is boring so your thoughts ramble.

But the next guest starts with: "Wait till I tell about this great little thing we did which increased our turnover by 30% last year. The company is flying now and it all began when…"

And what do you do? You lean in and turn up the sound, thinking: "I could do with some of that. I need to listen to this one".

The second guest is speaking normally and enthusiastically and is about to share a story about something real and understandable that is of complete interest to you and your world, so you pay attention.

Having the confidence to let go of formality and jargon and let your personality out of the bag, gives you the best chance of doing the kind of interview that connects.

And don't ever worry about your accent, your ums and aahs, and your personal mannerisms. These only become irritating if you have nothing to say. Forget about fishing for a bigger word to impress your mother. Just say what you have to say in a way that connects with us, and we won't notice your personal tics.

Managing Time

Time in an 'on air' studio has a special quality. It goes twice as fast as normal time. Not literally, but it feels that way.

You will usually be told, as a guest on a show, roughly how long the interview will run. So you will hear that they are taking you after the last ad break and before the news, and that it's a 5 or 6 minute slot; or they might say they will be coming to you at the top of the program, and you'll be getting about 15 minutes.

You prepare accordingly, and then it all changes. Because a Government Minister is suddenly available to talk about the interest rate hikes, and the presenter is told to finish up with you. Right now. Or even more scarily, the Jeremy Paxman scenario, where the Minister can't come into studio after all and the producer says: "Keep this interview going for another 10 minutes"!

So it is a moveable feast, and you have no idea where it is moving to next.

You manage the time by keeping your answers succinct. Remember the soccer analogy? It is very obvious when your response has scored a goal, and therefore it is very easy to stop there and invite another question in. The instinct to keep going or to ramble comes from knowing that you haven't quite nailed it yet.

The danger is that you will keep going over the one point, and suddenly the interview is over, and you haven't said half the things you wanted to say.

Another problem that inexperienced interviewees find is that they give hostages to fortune. The presenter 'takes a flier'. That is, he asks a question from way left of field in the hope that something interesting will emerge. You start into answering the question, although you know full well that the issue is not true and has nothing to do with you.

The clock is running down, and the whole of the rest of the interview can be spent on this issue that is of no relevance whatsoever, and was not what you went there that day to talk about.

Delivering the Message

Getting the business done is a very important part of any media encounter. Every programme and publication has a particular demographic attached, a core audience or readership that you can influence, or entertain, or persuade, depending on your purpose.

You do an interview not to fill time for the radio station, or fill column inches for the newspaper company, but to speak to your audience with a particular goal in mind.

It is very frustrating to leave a studio or walk away from an interview, knowing that you didn't quite do this. That you skirted around your issues, or got sidetracked, or got taken down an unfamiliar road, and completely wasted the opportunity.

To keep yourself on track, before the interview:

- Decide the one, two or three key messages you want to get across
- Decide the stories or anecdotes you can convincingly attach to each message
- Vocalize your stories so they can be told tightly and to the point

After that try to really listen to the interviewer's question, watching out for multi-part questions.

Do your preparation well, so that you know your material, but then try to leave the notes behind. If you have notes, you will instinctively keep scanning them, missing out on what the interviewer is saying. Whereas if you trust yourself to go without the notes, you will be fully in the zone, and paying attention to what is going on.

Having the Last Word

You can improve the overall 'score' of a live interview dramatically by finishing strongly. The last few sentences or piece of interest within any exchange creates the after-view, the sense the listener has of what the whole thing has been about.

You get this opportunity by taking it.

Interviewers are always hard-pressed for time, up against a clock, hurrying interviewees because of an ad break, or a promo, or a news bulletin. But the point is, why have they invited you into studio at all if they have no time for you?

Sometimes it is a genuine pressure they are under, but other times it is a bit of an affectation, a device to keep pace in the programme.

The give-away is when the presenter says he is out of time and then proceeds to ask you three more questions.

So in the same way that you have your parachute ready to finish a live presentation, have a strong point up your sleeve ready to finish up an interview.

As the interviewer is wrapping up, ask can you make one more point, and use the opportunity to make a final punchy statement or appeal, and to leave the listener with a vital piece of information about how to contact you or find out more.

～

Most of the examples here are framed in the scenario of a live interview for radio or television, and undoubtedly that kind of interview would be the most pressurised. But the techniques are just the same when the interview is for an online journal or for a newspaper.

You often end up doing those interviews by telephone from the comfort of your own desk or home, and it can be easy to be lulled into a false sense of security, and to make the mistake of rambling off on a tangent.

The best advice is to bear in mind all the points we have discussed here, and to keep to a few clear and well prepared messages, illustrated with strong examples.

And of course to get some good training if you are planning on starring on a primetime show any time soon.

Chapter Ten

Staying Focussed

*Finally, I want to share with you a few ideas
on motivation, the things that get us out of
bed in the morning, keep us going when things
are tough, and make us stay focused on all the
wonderful possibilities yet to come.*

Becoming a great workplace communicator is a challenge – yet another bar to clear when you have so many out there in front of you already. But of all the goals you might set yourself, the ones we have talked about here are probably the most achievable, and definitely completely within your own control.

These are ones you can start working on whenever you are ready, putting simple techniques into place and quickly getting results.

But to get going on your plan, you have to think about what inspires you. What drives you to put in that extra effort.

Virgin Group founder, Richard Branson, commenting on LinkedIn, wrote: "My professional inspiration has no separation from my personal inspiration: It is the people who will stop at nothing to make a positive difference to other people's lives. I am fortunate to come across quite a few of these game-changing people, and the desire to help (and keep up with them!) is what drives me."

I thought it very interesting that a man with Branson's profile and track record – to whom, no doubt, thousands of people look to every day for direction – finds his own motivation from people he meets who want to give back or make a difference. And he has the humility to say that he is trying to keep up with those people, not the other way around.

Writers will always tell you that they have to change their environment when they get stuck. Staring at the computer won't clear the logjam but going for a walk or climbing a mountain just might do the trick. The inspiration they are looking for is then triggered by a random encounter with another walker, or a spectacular view, or simply by getting the blood flowing and allowing a re-oxygenated brain to do its job.

I first heard the theory of the Cybernetic Loop at a media masterclass I attended in Cape Town a few years back called the Entertainment Masterclass, and it was so impactful.

Former comedian Paul Boross, now a successful author and business coach, came bounding into the training room and shook up our thinking with his energy and vitality. I know I wasn't the only one who took it fully on board, and have been living it ever since.

"I first discovered the idea of the cybernetic loop as a performer at The Comedy Store in London," he recalls. "It is renowned as the toughest place for comedians in the UK to perform because the audience are encouraged to heckle and harass the performers. I noticed that comedians (including many who went on to become household names) could control their chances of winning the audience over merely by how they prepared their physiology backstage.

"Comedians who stood up straight with shoulders back as they were about to go on stage automatically acted more confidently, took control and won respect from the crowd.

"I found that if I kept a good posture, lifted my chin and smiled, even though I was scared inside, it changed the way I thought about the whole performance. As I walked onto stage like a gladiator entering the ring, I felt an inward calmness and I found myself more able to tame the baying crowd.

"I realised that my physiology had a massive impact on my psychology and started to develop the technique so that I could not only use it to change my own feelings and perceptions, but also to help other people control theirs."

Ninety five per cent of your emotions – both positive and negative – are influenced by how you talk to yourself, the little voice in your head that tells you that you are going to be great, or the one that keeps telling you that you are going to crash and burn.

So it's not the things that happen to you but the way you interpret these events, and what you tell yourself about them, that determine how you feel at any given time. Then, how you feel completely influences how you respond, and what your body language is saying loudly to all those around you.

If you are sitting in a bit of a slump, feeling sorry for yourself, mentally exhausted, you need to physically change something in order that your brain can respond.

And in the same way, if you are physically energised, your brain will then fire better.

To my complete delight, I saw a fantastic manifestation of the theory when chairing the Pendulum Summit in the National Convention Centre in Dublin.

By mid afternoon the energy had left the room. The 2,000 delegates, listening since 8.30am were flagging, so I needed to do something to energise them before the headline act, Deepak Chopra. But we were running well over time, so it would have to be something quick! I whispered to Norma Murphy, the floor manager, to trust me and I started into a little exercise.

I asked everyone to stand up, and then to slump over, hanging their shoulders and their heads down, and to say in the lowest, saddest voice they could muster, "I am very happy."

It was actually great fun to see the whole convention obliging, going along with me, without knowing where this was going.

And then I asked them to throw their arms in the air, to stretch up as far as they could go, and to shout at the tops of their voices "I am very sad".

Well if you are so sad, I asked them, why are you all laughing?

And indeed, people were laughing, probably at the silliness of the exercise, but also appreciative of the change in the whole atmosphere in the room.

We each have to find the things that work for us – the energiser, the mood changer, the uplifter – the action that allows us to disconnect the cogs, and to go off in a different direction or at a different speed when we reconnect the cogs. And if for you that doesn't happen to be fresh air and exercise it can be:

- Taking a class in something new, like Japanese or economics

- Creating a vision board, or painting a picture

- Helping out a local charity

- Doing something for a friend in need

- Writing in your journal

- Watching an inspiring TED talk

- Reading a great book

- Making a bucket list

- Making a gratitude list

- Facetiming your four year old niece!

The point is that oscillation between activities allows us to be more productive.

'All work and no play makes Jack a dull boy,' so the old saying goes, and undoubtedly repeating the same activities over and over will drain us and leave us with that feeling of running on empty. The more we try to fit into an already over-crowded day, the less we are likely to actually get done.

Francesco Cirillo's Pomodoro Technique is a great one to try if you ever suffer from a feeling of disgruntlement at the end of a long and difficult day, that you didn't quite achieve enough, despite your best efforts.

The technique uses a red tomato shaped timer – physical or online, whichever you prefer – to allow you to really focus in a concentrated way for a short burst of time, and then to give your self that oscillation in the form of a short break, mental and physical.

So you set the timer for 25 minutes, and concentrate furiously on the task at hand – the report you are trying to write, the project that has to be completed, and when the timer goes off you stop completely, note what you have achieved and take a three to five minute break. The break should involve walking away from the task, and doing a few stretches or something else to pump the blood.

After four pomodori, or 25 minute work segments, you take a longer break of 15 to 30 minutes. Devotees of the technique swear by it, and have noticed huge increases in their productivity.

Author and speaker Dr Heidi Hanna has taken the concept of oscillation to another level with her research on brain training for optimal performance and output. In her books *The Sharp Solution* and *Stressoholic* she details how too much stress and not enough recovery time – along with poor diet, not enough exercise, and not enough real connection with those around us – actually causes the destruction of the brain.

And she spells out programmes you can put in place to get your brain into a better place to withstand the pressures of modern day living through recovery, rebalancing and recharging.

"Everything about the human system is designed

to oscillate – from heartbeats to brainwaves and blood sugar," she explains.

"Yet most people flat-line their way throughout the day, overriding our natural patterns in an attempt to get more done in less time.

"As a result, we depend on stress hormones and stimulation to keep our systems energised which ultimately causes us to break down and burnout. The simple solution is to manage energy more effectively by living life as a series of sprints rather than a marathon. Studies have shown that breaks as short as 3-5 minutes can help to balance brain chemistry, build brain health and boost brainpower!"

I have found Heidi's work in this area absolutely fascinating, and the best argument for minding the diet and taking more exercise I have ever come across – the positive gains in performance and output a much better carrot than any notions of air-brushed perfection.

But of course the knowing/doing gap features in here again. We all know what we should be doing, but actually getting around to doing it is another thing entirely, unless you are very disciplined.

"Like many CEOs I used to be a workaholic, confronting all of life's problems with the belief that I could fix them with more hours at the office", says Rory Geoghegan, of Red Box Direct. "But fostering a culture of long hours wasn't good for my business, staff, family or for myself – so I changed.

"I discovered exercise and how it could make me more productive. Now I hit the gym in the middle of every day and return to the office invigorated. Post-lunch used to be a grind. Now I get the buzzing energy of the morning twice every day.

"The realisation that being present and being productive are not the same thing has been an eye-opener and as a result I have become uncompromising in my commitment to my exercise programme. Now I have time for work, my family and for me. It all gets done!"

Psychologists will say that some people naturally have more resilience than others, but will equally argue that we can all develop more of it. It all depends on how much we accept that adversity is a normal part of life, and how much we are prepared or able to adjust to new circumstances, and look for the good in them.

So if we are to be healthily resilient, and confident, we have to accept the bad but balance it with the good, training the little voice in the head to say that this part of my life may be in shreds, but I still have this and this and this to be thankful about.

In *Flourishing*, psychologist and writer Maureen Gaffney, describes the 5:1 ratio of good experiences to bad we need to really thrive in life. Every little niggle or worry or put-down or call from a bank is a negative that needs to be countered with three indications of affection, or pleasant thoughts about an upcoming event or holiday, or signs of appreciation from someone. And that's just to keep us on an even keel!

To really flourish we need to find five positives to balance each negative. And we can't rely on others for the positives. We have to find ways of giving ourselves the positives, without resorting to chocolate or wine!

This can be done by reminding ourselves every day of the things we should be grateful for. Yes, it is a bit of a social media cliché at the moment to post 'gratitude' notes but there is science behind it, so it is not as corny as it looks. Consciously noting and appreciating the good things as we go along makes us emotionally stronger, more confident, and better able to withstand the bad things.

A constantly cheerful business development coach I know has a 'gratitude' file on the left of her screen, in there with all the projects she is currently working on. Every time she gets stressed, or feels it is all coming at her like a train, she opens the file, reads some of the things she has put there before, and adds in a new one.

She swears it immediately drops her blood pressure, focuses her, and allows her return to her tasks ready to go again. And the best thing is that kind of break has no calories!

Resilience is also fostered by a willingness to learn and an openness to new things. None of us is ever fully 'cooked'. We are works in progress, and the day you decide you know it all is the day you start to make the road really long and hard for yourself.

Instead, if you start looking for learning in everything, even the bad stuff, you are training your brain for adaptability and agility, and ultimately happiness and success.

So you might ask yourself what have I learned from this situation? What do I now know about myself that I didn't before? How can I use this experience into the future? How can I make sure that others don't have to face what I did?

Learning to deal with stuff is what makes us who we are. Every challenge we have successfully overcome has grown our confidence, strengthened our will, given us the notion that we can tackle things head on in the future – qualities we would never have developed if we had not had the difficulties in the first place.

I sometimes think that the only thing we really, really need to give our children is the ability to solve problems, because if they can do that, everything else will fall into place. If we can get them to believe that they probably *will* be able to work out what to do, in most sets of circumstances, they will be unstoppable.

And that's not to say they should have an unrealistic belief in their abilities, but more that they should trust themselves to cope with whatever might come along, and not to be pole-axed with shock that bad things are out there in the first place.

Another big part of developing and fostering confidence and resilience is a healthy and active community; the people who are there for you, who have your back, and who share and understand your experiences. There are friends you have a laugh with, friends you have a moan with, friends you drink too many cocktails with, and friends who support you, and we need them all.

Social media is a lot of fun, and a great way to create some 'white noise' around your product or service, but it also alienates people and creates a lot of loneliness – every one else appearing to have a happier, glossier, more successful life than your own.

But life is not a see-saw. You are not down because someone else is up. So there is no need to let pictures of weddings and exotic travel and successful people incite Tik-Tok envy. Or no need to let social media weaken your resilience muscle.

Use it instead to find and share stories of people who have overcome great odds, and who inspire us every day with their own positivity, adaptability and refusal to let adversity hold them back.

I once heard ambitions and goals described as shiny pennies, and I thought it was very apt. You have to scatter them there on the table in front of you, and play around with them until you can see some order, until they start to stack up, and things fall into place for you.

So you do a brain dump of all the things you want to do – like writing the book, or recording the song, or running the marathon, or changing the job – putting down everything that comes into your head with absolutely no self-limits or self-doubt allowed.

These are the shiny pennies, and the list could be quite long and quite out there!

But by simply writing the list, you are admitting to yourself that you do actually want these things, and there is a part of your brain telling you loudly that you are quite capable of achieving them.

So now you have to decide in what order are you going to tackle the things on the list. Or in other words, which of the pennies is the shiniest, the most appealing, the closest to your heart? Which of the things do you really want to go after now? And where is the ladder that is going to lead to that goal?

Doing some communications training with a group of aspiring politicians, I asked them to discuss ambition. It took quite a bit of pushing, but eventually a few of them admitted that they would quite like to be Prime Minister one day.

So I drew a ladder on the flip chart, put the words Prime Minister on the top, and we started working out the rungs of the ladder going down – party leader, government minister, junior minister, elected representative, party convention nominee, party member, local representative, student politics and so on.

Some of the group was not even on the first rung of the ladder then, but the exercise was useful for them, and they could see clearly what they had to do. Don't get put off by how far away the top of the mountain is, concentrate on getting up to the next ledge.

And you are far more likely to get the help and support you need to climb to the next ledge, if you are looking, acting and sounding like a strong communicator and potential leader, long before you actually reach that pay grade.

Body language, personal mannerisms and the way we use language can sometimes give away personal power. Aspiring leaders need to avoid the signals that display unease or lack of confidence to others.

The physical signals that reduce the perception of personal power include poor posture, lack of eye contact, shifting weight from foot to foot, looking stressed or harried, touching the face or playing with the hair.

The verbal signals include things like deflecting compliments, self-deprecation, confiding insecurities, speaking too fast or too slow, taking too long to get to the point and using hesitant or weak language.

The opposite is of course to practise giving out strong verbal and physical signals which protect your personal power.

This includes taking credit where it is due, knowing what you want and asking for it, using decisive language, speaking up, having clear views, understanding the difference between assertiveness and aggression, knowing when to say no, and understanding the sources and uses of power within the group or organisation.

Remember Paul Boross's advice above about getting your physiology right? Some people call this 'faking it till you make it' or in other words, acting the way you want to be perceived. Because if you act like you are confident, and know what you are talking about, you will firstly be perceived in that way, and then you will actually become that way.

And taking that logic forward, if you act like a confident communicator you will be perceived as one, and you will eventually become one.

But no matter how big your ambitions are, don't ever let them distract you from giving your all at your current level. You get promoted because of how well you are doing your current role, not because you are letting everyone know you are not focusing on it, because you really believe you are too good for it.

Acting confidently means delivering results daily, so that nobody around you – above, below or to the side – has reason to ever question your performance. It means offering to carry an extra load, taking on additional projects that are in themselves fulfilling but which also signal your potential.

It's about finding role models and mentors within the group, and working to support their projects and goals so you can learn from them.

It's about finding and recognising your blind spots, so you get some training and development in those areas, or at very least you can find work-arounds, until the time comes when you can employ someone to do that aspect of the work.

It's about networking and building strong relationships so that people already know what you are like and what you are capable of, long before you sit across from them at the interview board.

❧

The path to becoming a confident communicator is wide open to anyone who chooses to take it. Achieving that elusive executive presence, or the kind of gravitas that makes people listen to and really connect with what you are saying, is completely achievable. By you. Now.

But it takes dedication, plenty of practice and a little luck. And remember, the harder you work, the luckier you get.

The funny thing is that those who get there usually never really accept that they have done so. They are committed to life-long learning and continuous self-development, so they are always looking to nudge their personal bar just that little bit higher.

Thank you for reading *Speak Now*, and I hope to meet you in person some day to hear about your own road to success.

About the Author

Orlaith Carmody is an expert communications consultant, executive coach and author.

She has delivered keynotes, coaching and training for many years, nationally and internationally, and has facilitated high level workshops and strategy days all over the world.

Following an early career as a broadcast journalist with Irish National station RTÉ, she became a director of a number of SMEs in media, production, recruitment, and education, and served on the boards of RTÉ, the Broadcasting Authority of Ireland, and a number of charities and social enterprises.

Orlaith is a Senior Practitioner with the European Mentoring and Coaching Council (EMCC); a Fellow of the Learning and Development Institute (FLDI) and a Certified Management Consultant (CMC). She has an MA in Communications from Dublin City university.

Find out more about the author at her own website: www.OrlaithCarmody.com

Acknowledgements

A big thanks to long-time friend and writer Helena Mulkerns for encouraging me to take a hard look at my first book, *Perform as a Leader*, and to re-purpose it completely for a brand new audience.

Thanks also to PJ Cunningham of Ballpoint Press who nursed the original to completion; to my ace sense checkers this time around - Cormac Duffy, Dearbhla Gallagher and Brian Coleman; to my family for the understanding and the support when I keep disappearing into the study and closing the door; and to my gorgeous dogs, terrier Cailean and labrador Johnny for keeping me company.

Finally to my husband of nearly thirty years, Gavin Duffy, heartfelt thanks for the continuous inspiration, love and support.